Best Easy Day Hikes
Shenandoah National Park

Help Us Keep This Guide Up to Date

Every effort has been made by the authors and editors to make this guide as accurate and useful as possible. However, many things can change after a guide is published—trails are rerouted, regulations change, techniques evolve, facilities come under new management, etc.

We would appreciate hearing from you concerning your experiences with this guide and how you feel it could be improved and kept up to date. While we may not be able to respond to all comments and suggestions, we'll take them to heart, and we'll also make certain to share them with the authors. Please send your comments and suggestions to the following address:

FalconGuides
Reader Response/Editorial Department
246 Goose Lane
Guilford, CT 06437

Or you may e-mail us at: editorial@falcon.com

Thanks for your input, and happy trails!

Best Easy Day Hikes Series

Best Easy Day Hikes
Shenandoah
National Park

Fifth Edition

Bert and Jane Gildart

FALCONGUIDES

GUILFORD, CONNECTICUT
HELENA, MONTANA

FALCONGUIDES®

An imprint of Rowman & Littlefield
Falcon and FalconGuides are registered trademarks and Make Adventure Your Story is a trademark of Rowman & Littlefield.

Distributed by NATIONAL BOOK NETWORK

Copyright © 2016 by Rowman & Littlefield

Maps: Maps by XNR Productions, Ltd. © Rowman & Littlefield

British Library Cataloguing-in-Publication Information Available

Library of Congress Cataloging-in-Publication Data Available

ISBN 978-1-4930-1686-0 (pbk. : alk. paper)
ISBN 978-1-4930-1687-7 (e-book)

∞™ The paper used in this publication meets the minimum requirements of American National Standard for Information Sciences—Permanence of Paper for Printed Library Materials, ANSI/NISO Z39.48-1992.

Contents

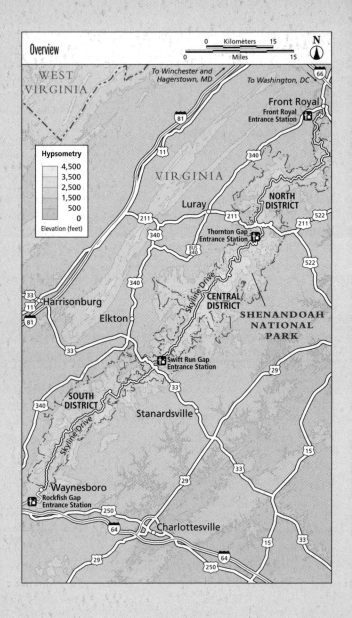

South District

Acknowledgments

No book is ever written and completed without the help of others, and this guide is no exception. First, we'd like to thank Steve Bair and Melissa Rudacille, both park rangers at Shenandoah National Park, who reviewed the book and provided much valuable information. We attempted to incorporate all of their thoughts, suggestions, and ideas and hope we have interpreted their comments correctly. As well, we'd like to thank Greta Miller, director of the Shenandoah National Park Association, and Dan Hurlbert, the park's map specialist, who simplified the verification of GPS coordinates with map overlays. Greta aided with initial logistics and helped us establish just what direction our work would follow.

We want to thank Adam and Susan Maffei for companionship in 2010 as we rehiked many of the park's trails. They are special friends and quintessential hikers. We also want to thank Julie Marsh, who has helped us not only with early editions of this publication but several other FalconGuides as well. She has an eagle eye and the patience of Job. The same applies to Lynn Zelem, editor on this, our most recent edition. She has recognized features that time might have changed in the Shenandoah landscape and made sure our text remains appropriate.

Finally, our thanks to Bill Schneider, founder of Falcon Press, who got us to Shenandoah way back in 1998, and to both Jessica Haberman and Katie Benoit of Globe Pequot Press, who have gotten us back years later for successive editions.

Introduction

Shenandoah National Park straddles a beautiful stretch of the Blue Ridge, which forms the eastern rampart of the Appalachian Mountains. Beginning in the late 1700s, settlers drifted into these hills and "hollers." They cleared some of the vast forests that originally blanketed the region so that they could till the land. Shenandoah was established as a national park in 1935. For the most part, the forests reestablished naturally. As the flora returned, so did Shenandoah's fauna. Today, some 200 species of birds occupy the park, as well as around fifty species of mammals, some of which had declined significantly in number prior to the park's establishment.

Today, Shenandoah offers a little something for everyone with an interest in the out-of-doors. The park attracts 1.2 million visitors annually and, to accommodate these crowds, is open 24 hours a day, seven days a week, unless the roads are closed due to ice, snow, or fog. Two visitor centers—Dickey Ridge in the North District and Byrd Visitor Center at Big Meadows—are open seven days a week from 8:30 a.m. to 5 p.m. beginning about the first of April and usually closing in late November. For current park information, call headquarters at (540) 999-3500; write to Shenandoah National Park, 3655 US Highway 211 E, Luray, VA 22835; or visit www.nps.gov/shen.

As a further means of accommodating visitors, the park has four public campgrounds with a total of 660 campsites. Big Meadow closes at the end of November, while the other three close October 31. There are no hookups for RVs, but water and dump stations as well as restrooms are available. Propane and diesel fuel are not available in the park, only in surrounding towns.

1

In some of the campgrounds, some sites are allocated on a first-come, first-served basis. Getting a spot can be difficult, particularly in the summer and in the fall, when autumn foliage peaks. At Big Meadows, Mathews Arm, and Loft Mountain campgrounds make reservations for mid-May through October. Even if you arrive during the week and get a spot, there is some chance you might have to move as the weekend rolls around, because visitors with reservations have priority. At Lewis Mountain Campground sites are on a first-come, first-served basis.

Dogs on a 6-foot leash are allowed on most trails throughout the park. A few trails do not permit dogs. See "Canine compatibility" for each hike.

Though Shenandoah offers many attractions, hikes to the waterfalls and highest peaks remain among the most popular. Fortunately, access to these most scenic of attractions is relatively easy.

Getting There

Shenandoah is easily accessible from a variety of different locales. In the north you can access the park via Front Royal, Virginia, by leaving US 340 south of town and following the bold and abundant signs to the park's entrance. From the highway, the park's northern entrance station is less than a mile away.

From the south, you can access the park by driving from Waynesboro via US 250 to the Rockfish Gap entrance station. You can also enter at its Thornton Gap entrance, 30 miles farther north, via US 211. If you are coming through Harrisonburg to the west or Stanardsville to the east, you can enter on US 33 at the Swift Run Gap entrance. From

Charlottesville and Richmond, you can take I-64 west to Rockfish Gap, the park's southernmost entrance.

Once in the park, you will drive the famous Skyline Drive. Along the west side of this 105.4-mile route, the park has conveniently placed mile markers. Because almost all trails radiate from Skyline Drive, it's very simple to find your desired trailhead. The mileposts begin just after the north entrance of the park, accessed from the town of Front Royal. The last marker, Milepost 105.4, is located at Rockfish Gap in the south. From here, the Blue Ridge Parkway continues south; the town of Waynesboro is at the base of the mountains as you leave the park.

On your road map you may notice that Skyline Drive does not run precisely north and south. However, for purposes of this guidebook, all directions assume that as you drive from the north end of the park to the south end, east will be on your left and west will be to your right.

What Is a "Best Easy" Hike?

While researching and writing a much larger FalconGuide called *Hiking Shenandoah*, we had frequent discussions with rangers about what kind of information hikers most often requested. We also had the same type of discussion with many hikers on the trails.

It seems there are two general types of visitors: those who want to spend several days exploring Shenandoah's backcountry and those who will be in the park only a day or two and would like a choice sampling of its special features. This book is for the second group.

The more comprehensive book, *Hiking Shenandoah*, covers nearly every trail in the park, including those that are neither best nor easy. *Best Easy Day Hikes* includes only short, less-strenuous hikes that we consider among the nicest day hikes in the park. None have drastically long climbs.

Some of the hikes in this book might seem easy to some but not to others. To help you decide which are for you, we have ranked the hikes from easiest to hardest below. Please keep in mind that short does not always equal easy. Other factors such as elevation gain and trail conditions have to be considered.

We hope you enjoy your "best easy" hiking in Shenandoah National Park!

Ranking the Hikes

The following list ranks the hikes in this book from easiest to more challenging. The milepost numbers correspond to those displayed along Skyline Drive and indicate the hike's location on this, the main route through the park.

12	Limberlost, Skyline Drive Mile 43.0
16	Story of the Forest Trail, Skyline Drive Mile 51.0
4	Fort Windham Rocks, Skyline Drive Mile 10.4
1	Fox Hollow Trail, Skyline Drive Mile 4.6
2	Snead Farm, Skyline Drive Mile 5.1
5	Traces Trail, Skyline Drive Mile 22.2
24	Loft Mountain Loop, Skyline Drive Mile 79.5
25	Blackrock Summit, Skyline Drive Mile 84.8
26	Calvary and Chimney Rocks, Skyline Drive Mile 90.0
27	Calf Mountain, Skyline Drive Mile 99.5
20	Pocosin Trail, Skyline Drive Mile 59.5
11	Millers Head, Skyline Drive Mile 42.5
3	Lands Run Falls, Skyline Drive Mile 9.2

Leave No Trace

Visiting a national park such as Shenandoah is like going to a famous art museum. Obviously, you do not want to leave your mark on an art treasure in the museum. If every visitor to the museum left one little mark, the piece of art would quickly be destroyed—and of what value is a big building full of trashed art? The same goes for a wilderness such as Shenandoah National Park, which is as magnificent and as valuable as any masterpiece by any artist. If we all left one little mark on the landscape, the wilderness would soon be despoiled.

A wilderness can accommodate plenty of human use as long as everybody behaves. But a few thoughtless or uninformed visitors can ruin it for everybody who follows. The need for good manners applies to all wilderness users, not just hikers.

Leave No Trace Principles

- Plan ahead and prepare.
- Travel and camp on durable surfaces.
- Dispose of waste properly.
- Leave what you find.
- Minimize campfire impact.
- Respect wildlife.
- Be considerate of other visitors.

For more details, visit www.LNT.org.

Most of us know better than to litter—in or out of the wilderness. Be sure you leave nothing, regardless of how small it is, along the trail or at your campsite. This means that you should pack out everything, including orange peels, flip-tops, cigarette butts, and gum wrappers. You may even want to pick up any obvious trash others have dropped along the way.

Follow the main trail. Avoid cutting switchbacks and walking on vegetation beside the trail. In the mountains some terrain is very fragile, so stay on the trail.

Don't pick up souvenirs, such as rocks, antlers, or wildflowers. And remember, here in Shenandoah you must go even further. Should you see old bedsprings or other items discarded by the mountain people of yesteryear, leave them as you found them. Park officials regard them as historic artifacts.

Avoid making loud noises that may disturb others. Remember, sound travels easily along the ridges and through the canyons. Be courteous.

Bury human waste 6 to 8 inches deep and pack out used toilet paper. This is a good reason to carry a lightweight trowel. Keep waste at least 300 feet away from any water source.

Finally, and perhaps most importantly, strictly follow the pack-in and pack-out rule. If you carry something into the backcountry, consume it or carry it out.

About the Maps

The maps in this book use elevation tints, called hypsometry, to portray relief. Each gray tone represents a range of equal elevation, as shown in the scale key with the map. The darker tones are lower elevations and the lighter grays are higher elevations. Narrow bands of different gray tones spaced closely together indicate steep terrain, whereas wider bands indicate areas of more gradual slope.

Map Legend

81	Interstate
11	U.S. Highway
231	State Highway
604	Local Road
- - - - - - -	Unpaved Road
▬▬▬▬▬▬	Featured Trail
- - - - - - -	Trail
⌇	River/Creek
- ·· - ·· -	Intermittent Stream
⌇	Marsh
⌐	Spring
⋙	Waterfall
⌐ ⌐	National Park
⌐⌐⌐⌐	Rock Outcrop Management Plan (ROMP) Area
‿	Bridge
▲	Camping
⊤⊤⊤⊤⊤	Cliffs
•—•—	Gate
⚘	Horse Trail
▲	Mountain Peak
🅿	Parking
⌣	Pass/Gap
⌖	Picnic Area
■	Point of Interest/Structure
🛈	Ranger Station
○	Town
❶	Trailhead
🗻	Viewpoint/Overlook
❓	Visitor/Information Center

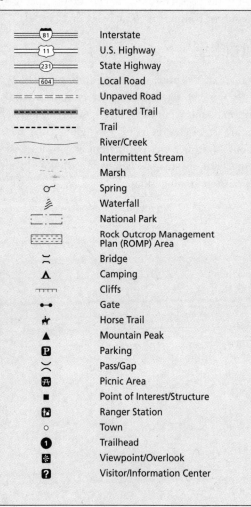

North District

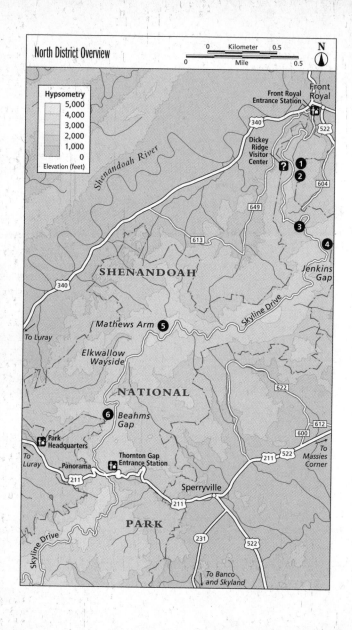

North District Overview

Hypsometry
5,000
4,000
3,000
2,000
1,000
0
Elevation (feet)

Kilometer
0   0.5
Mile
0   0.5

N

Front Royal Entrance Station
Front Royal
340
522
Dickey Ridge Visitor Center
604
Shenandoah River
649
613
3
4
Jenkins Gap
SHENANDOAH
340
Skyline Drive
To Luray
Mathews Arm 5
Elkwallow Wayside
NATIONAL
622
6 Beahms Gap
612
Park Headquarters
600
To Massies Corner
Panorama
Thornton Gap Entrance Station
211
522
211
To Luray
Sperryville
PARK
Skyline Drive
231
522
To Banco and Skyland

1 Fox Hollow Trail

This short and easy loop makes a delightful history hike to an old homestead area. An interpretive pamphlet, available for a small fee at the Dickey Ridge Visitor Center, will enhance the hike. The trail is not rough and is suitable for children. Blue blazes mark the trail.

Start: Skyline Drive Mile 4.6, Dickey Ridge Visitor Center
Trailhead GPS: N38 52.307' / W78 12.221'
Type of hike: Loop
Distance: 1.2 miles
Hiking time: 30 to 60 minutes
Difficulty: Easy to moderate

Elevation gain and loss: 310 feet
Canine compatibility: Dogs not allowed
Maps: National Geographic Trails Illustrated Topo Map 228; *Map 9, Appalachian Trail and Other Trails in Shenandoah National Park, North District* (PATC, Inc.)

The Hike

Begin the hike on the east side of Skyline Drive, across from the Dickey Ridge Visitor Center. The kiosk provides further information about the area and serves as the trailhead. The clockwise trail begins with a slight descent and accesses Dickey Ridge Trail to the left at a cement post at about 0.15 mile. Turn left and follow the blue-blazed trail for 0.2 mile. At the cement post at 0.3 mile, turn right at the fork onto Fox Hollow Trail, also blue-blazed, past piles of rocks reflecting the work once required to clear the forest and prepare it for cultivation.

At 0.5 mile the trail passes Fox Farm Cemetery. The largest stone memorializes Lemuel F. Fox, the son of Thomas

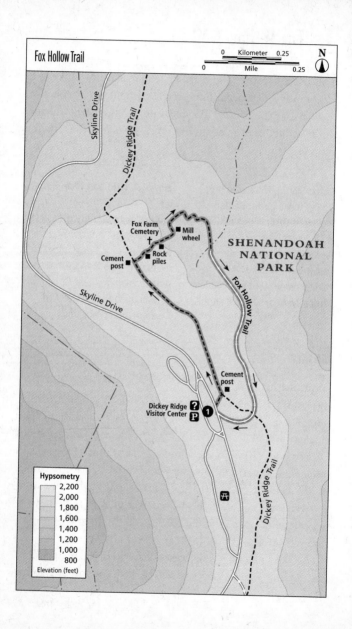

Fox Hollow Trail

Kilometer 0.25
Mile 0.25

N

Skyline Drive

Dickey Ridge Trail

Fox Farm Cemetery

Mill wheel

Rock piles

Cement post

Skyline Drive

SHENANDOAH NATIONAL PARK

Fox Hollow Trail

Cement post

Dickey Ridge Visitor Center

1

Dickey Ridge Trail

Hypsometry

2,200
2,000
1,800
1,600
1,400
1,200
1,000
800

Elevation (feet)

Fox, who established the family farm here in 1856. According to the inscription, Lemuel died May 24, 1916, at the age of 78. The trail continues to descend gradually, passing a spring and a mill wheel once used for ornamental purposes. The trail continues to cross old farmland now being reclaimed by the forest. Deer have returned to the area and now abound.

Shortly after passing the cemetery, the trail begins its return to the visitor center by climbing gradually. Along the trail, rock piles and rock fences continue to proclaim that farming once dominated the area. The path is actually an old road that once linked the Fox family with the town of Front Royal. At mile 1.1 stay straight at the cement post marking Dickey Ridge Trail to return to the trailhead.

Miles and Directions

0.0 Park kiosk on east side of Skyline Drive, at Dickey Ridge Visitor Center.

0.15 Cement post; turn left onto blue-blazed Dickey Ridge Trail.

0.3 Cement post; take right fork east onto blue-blazed Fox Hollow Trail.

0.35 First of many rock piles.

0.5 Fox Farm Cemetery; continue south on Fox Hollow Trail.

1.1 Shortly after mile 1.1, cement post marks the Dickey Ridge Trail (blue-blazed) going north–south. Do not turn—stay straight.

1.2 Arrive back at trailhead.

2 Snead Farm

Appropriate for families, this hike takes you to buildings used by the Snead family when they homesteaded in the area. It was active between the 1850s and 1960s, at which time the final land owners sold the farm to the park.

Start: Skyline Drive Mile 5.1. This trail can be accessed at the end of Fox Hollow Trail by turning left onto Dickey Ridge Trail. Or cross Skyline Drive to the east, opposite the exit for the Dickey Ridge picnic area. You can park at either the visitor center or the south end of the picnic area.
Trailhead GPS: N38 52.307' / W78 12.221'
Type of hike: Loop

Distance: 3.2 miles
Hiking time: About 2 hours
Difficulty: Easy
Elevation gain and loss: 500 feet
Canine compatibility: Dogs allowed
Maps: National Geographic Trails Illustrated Topo Map 228; Map 9, Appalachian Trail and Other Trails in Shenandoah National Park, North District (PATC, Inc.)

The Hike

The visit to Snead Farm is a trip back in time. At one time the owners worked this 200-acre piece of land as farmland and as an apple orchard. The park bought the land in 1962. The remnants here are quite visible; the barn still stands, as does the root cellar. The stone remains of an old house fill an open area. With but little imagination, you can recognize the difficulty these people had in clearing and farming this land.

After accessing Snead Farm Road, continue straight (south) at the intersection with Dickey Ridge Trail, left at the second fork, and right at the last fork. The walk to the farm

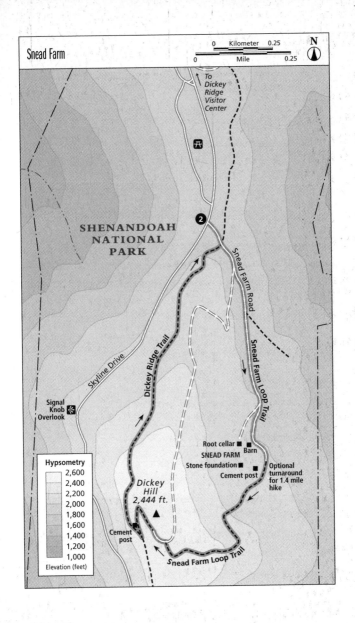

Snead Farm

N

To
Dickey
Ridge
Visitor
Center

2

SHENANDOAH
NATIONAL
PARK

Snead Farm Road

Dickey Ridge Trail

Snead Farm Loop Trail

Skyline Drive

Signal
Knob
Overlook

Root cellar ■
SNEAD FARM   ■ Barn
Stone foundation ■
Cement post ■

Optional
turnaround
for 1.4 mile
hike

Dickey
Hill
2,444 ft.
▲

Cement
post

Snead Farm Loop Trail

Hypsometry

Elevation
2,600
2,400
2,200
2,000
1,800
1,600
1,400
1,200
1,000

Elevation (feet)

is a pleasant one along an old farm road. Upon reaching the farm at 0.7 mile, take time to explore the barn. Peer into the old root cellar; examine the stone foundation of the bunkhouse. (**Option:** From Snead Farm, you can turn around and retrace your steps to the picnic area for an out-and-back hike of 1.4 miles.)

To continue on the loop hike, access the blue-blazed Snead Farm Loop Trail, which continues at a cement post near the stone foundation at mile 0.7.

Hike about 1 mile to another cement post at a T junction with the Dickey Ridge Trail. Go right (north). The visitor center is 1.3 miles from this point.

The trail begins a slightly strenuous ascent to the top of Dickey Hill. At the summit take the spur trail to your right (north). For a marvelous view of Signal Knob on Massanutten Mountain and of the Shenandoah Valley, go left.

Retrace your steps to return to Dickey Ridge Trail. You will make another quick ascent. Then the trail begins to descend gradually beneath a canopy of trees. It continues through a quiet woods to an intersection with Snead Farm Road, completing the loop. A short walk to the left returns you to Skyline Drive near the picnic area.

Miles and Directions

0.0 Chain gate across drive from picnic area; stay on Snead Farm Road.

0.1 Intersect with Dickey Ridge Trail; continue straight on Snead Farm Road.

0.3 Fork in road; stay left.

0.5 Fork in road; stay right.

0.7 Remains of Snead Farm; access the Snead Farm Loop Trail from the cement post opposite the stone foundation; follow trail south (to your right as you face the post) toward another cement post to continue the loop hike. (**Option:** Turn around here and retrace your steps to the picnic area for a 1.4-mile hike.)

1.9 At cement post, turn right (north) onto the blue-blazed Dickey Ridge Trail.

3.2 Arrive at picnic area.

3 Lands Run Falls

An enjoyable jaunt down an old road leads to views of a pretty waterfall.

Start: Skyline Drive Mile 9.2, Lands Run parking area
Trailhead GPS: N38 50.0561' / W78 11.1371'
Type of hike: Out and back
Distance: 1.2 miles
Hiking time: 30 to 60 minutes
Difficulty: Easy

Elevation gain and loss: About 300 feet
Canine compatibility: Dogs allowed
Maps: National Geographic Trails Illustrated Topo Map 228; *Map 9, Appalachian Trail and Other Trails in Shenandoah National Park, North District* (PATC Inc.)

The Hike

Lands Run Falls is not especially high, nor can you see the entire falls from the trail. But the setting is lovely, and the trek provides a nice leg stretcher. Woods flanking the trail are dominated by oaks and hickories, interspersed with tulip poplars. Many of the healthiest oaks here were knocked down by Tropical Storm Fran in 1996. Those not already denuded by gypsy moths were so heavily laden with leaves that they were easily toppled by the strong winds. In addition to a lovely forest, there is a great deal of greenstone (volcanic rock) exposed by soil erosion. Look for greenstone on the uphill side of the road.

From the Lands Run parking area, follow the fire road, which descends immediately and continues to do so. At 0.6 mile a stream courses down the hill from the left and passes through a culvert under the road. The falls are on the right.

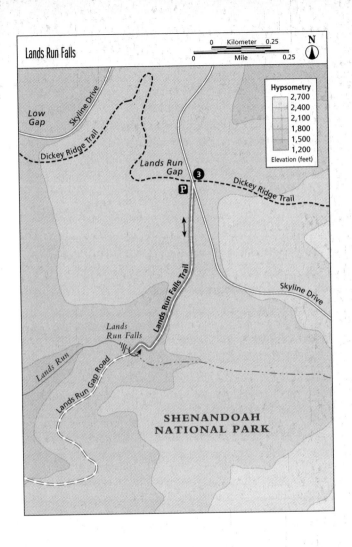

Lands Run Falls

Low
Gap

Skyline Drive

Dickey Ridge Trail

Lands Run
Gap

3
P

Dickey Ridge Trail

Skyline Drive

Lands Run Falls Trail

Lands
Run Falls

Lands Run

Lands Run Gap Road

SHENANDOAH
NATIONAL PARK

Hypsometry
2,700
2,400
2,100
1,800
1,500
1,200
Elevation (feet)

N

0   Kilometer   0.25
0   Mile   0.25

By taking a short spur trail to the right, you can get some inspiring views. The slickrock and precipitous grade create a potential hazard, so use caution.

Lands Run Gap Road continues for another 1.4 miles to the park boundary. Unless you have lots of energy to burn, there is not much point in continuing; the road descends another 600 feet with no viewpoints.

From the falls, turn around and retrace your steps—uphill, of course—including one short, steep portion to return to parking area.

Miles and Directions

0.0 Follow fire road at south end of Lands Run parking area.

0.6 Stream enters from left, waterfall on right. Turn around to retrace your steps.

1.2 Arrive at Lands Run parking area.

4 Fort Windham Rocks

A good leg stretcher, this hike offers photographic opportunities and insights into local geology.

Start: Skyline Drive Mile 10.4, Compton Gap; trail begins on the fire road / Appalachian Trail at the northeast end of the parking lot
Trailhead GPS: N38 49.487' / W78 10.10251'
Type of hike: Out and back
Distance: 0.8 mile
Hiking time: About 1 hour
Difficulty: Easy

Canine compatibility: Dogs allowed
Elevation gain and loss: Negligible
Maps: National Geographic Trails Illustrated Topographic Map 228; *Map 9, Appalachian Trail and Other Trails in Shenandoah National Park, North District* (PATC, Inc.)

The Hike

Begin the hike by walking from the parking lot, up the fire road / Appalachian Trail to a four-way junction. Turn left onto the Dickey Ridge Trail (blue blazes). The path ascends gently through a new-growth forest that offers ideal habitat for ruffed grouse and other wildlife. Several broods dashed across the trail as we hiked toward the rocks.

As the trail levels, the 45- to 50-foot Fort Windham Rocks appear on your right. Geologists tell us the rocks are 600 million to 800 million years old and are examples of the Catoctin lava formations. Follow the short spur on right side of trail, which leads into the rocks.

To return, retrace your steps back to the parking lot.

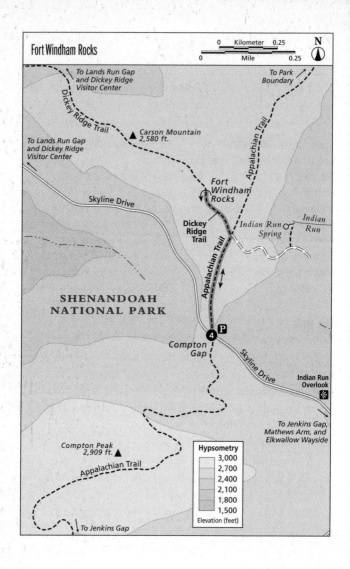

Fort Windham Rocks

0   Kilometer   0.25

0   Mile   0.25

N

To Lands Run Gap
and Dickey Ridge
Visitor Center

To Park
Boundary

Dickey Ridge Trail

▲ Carson Mountain
2,580 ft.

Appalachian Trail

To Lands Run Gap
and Dickey Ridge
Visitor Center

Skyline Drive

*Fort
Windham
Rocks*

**Dickey
Ridge
Trail**

*Indian Run
Spring*

*Indian
Run*

Appalachian Trail

**SHENANDOAH
NATIONAL PARK**

❹ Ⓟ

*Compton
Gap*

Skyline Drive

**Indian Run
Overlook**

To Jenkins Gap,
Mathews Arm, and
Elkwallow Wayside

Compton Peak
2,909 ft. ▲

Appalachian Trail

↓ To Jenkins Gap

Hypsometry	
	3,000
	2,700
	2,400
	2,100
	1,800
	1,500
Elevation (feet)	

Miles and Directions

0.0 From the parking lot, begin the hike at the fire road / AT.

0.2 Cement post, trail junction; go left on Dickey Ridge Trail.

0.4 High rocks on right; retrace your steps to return to the parking lot.

0.6 Turn right (south) onto the fire road / AT.

0.8 Arrive at parking lot.

Option: As you return, you might want to lengthen your hike by 0.6 mile to drop in at Indian Run Spring. This option will add maybe 45 minutes to your hike, depending on how long you spend at the spring. From the rocks, when you return to the fire road / AT, continue straight ahead at the cement post on the service road, heading downhill. Take the spur trail to your left to reach the spring. It offers cool water, which should be filtered or boiled before drinking. From here, retrace your steps to the AT; turn left (south) to return to the parking lot.

5 Traces Trail

This forest hike follows a trail that passes "traces" of mountain folk inhabitation and natural history.

Start: Skyline Drive Mile 22.2, east end of amphitheater parking lot, Mathews Arm Campground
Trailhead GPS: N38 42.599' / W78 17.834'
Type of hike: Loop
Distance: 1.7 miles
Hiking time: 1 to 3 hours, depending on your degree of fascination with cultural and natural history

Difficulty: Easy to moderate
Elevation gain and loss: Negligible
Canine compatibility: Dogs not allowed
Maps: National Geographic Trails Illustrated Topo Map 228; *Map 9, Appalachian Trail and Other Trails in Shenandoah National Park, North District* (PATC, Inc.)

The Hike

Because this trail climbs gently, you can probably complete this hike in an hour—if an hour is all the time you have. Packing much into a short distance, this is a great hike for families with small children as well as for people who can no longer hike as well as they once did. It should also appeal to anyone who has an interest in natural and cultural history. Along the trail you will see a lot of greenstone, a type of volcanic rock that was formed 800 million years ago. The trail is ideally located for the camper: It departs from Mathews Arm Campground and assumes a counterclockwise circle around the campground. Dogs are not allowed on this trail.

Access the trailhead from the east end of the parking lot, which serves the amphitheater to the right of the entrance

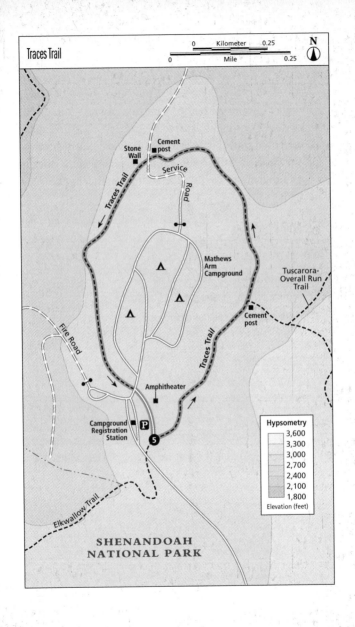

Traces Trail

Kilometer
0   0.25
Mile
0   0.25

N

Stone Wall

Cement post

Service Road

Traces Trail

Mathews Arm Campground

Tuscarora-Overall Run Trail

Fire Road

Cement post

Traces Trail

Amphitheater

Campground Registration Station

P

5

Elkwallow Trail

Hypsometry

3,600
3,300
3,000
2,700
2,400
2,100
1,800
Elevation (feet)

SHENANDOAH NATIONAL PARK

station. The trail is broad and begins beneath a mantle of red oak. Soon the trail climbs above the amphitheater. If the trail is wet, it may be slippery, so use caution. At the cement post at 0.4 mile, bear left. And at the cement post at 1 mile, go straight. Toward the end of your hike, there is a huge oak that for some reason was spared the ax. If trees could speak, this one could probably relate close to 200 years of history.

Near trail's end the forest canopy opens slightly, offering hints of other, more lofty vistas. Return to the amphitheater parking lot.

Miles and Directions

0.0 Sign at east end of amphitheater.

0.4 Cement post; stay left; descend.

1.0 Cement post; go straight.

1.7 Arrive at amphitheater parking lot.

6 Byrds Nest Summit and Byrds Nest Shelter No. 4

This is a fun, tranquil hike through a deciduous forest up to one of four day-use shelters in the park.

Start: Skyline Drive Mile 28.5, Beahms Gap parking area
Trailhead GPS: N38 41.7215' / W78 19.1998'
Type of hike: Out and back
Distance: 3.2 miles
Difficulty: Easy to moderate
Hiking time: About 2 hours

Canine compatibility: Dogs allowed
Elevation gain and loss: About 490 feet
Maps: National Geographic Trails Illustrated Topo Map 228; *Map 9, Appalachian Trail and Other Trails in Shenandoah National Park, North District* (PATC, Inc.)

The Hike

This short, relatively easy day hike takes you up to a ridge on the Neighbor Mountain Trail and to the Byrds Nest Shelter No. 4, a day-use shelter built in 1965. It is one of four shelters in the park constructed with donations from former senator Harry F. Byrd Sr. The trek is pretty and tranquil. On clear days you can see beyond Pass Mountain to the south. The shelter is a large, three-sided stone structure with a huge fireplace and picnic table.

Begin this hike at the cement post at the north end of the Beahms Gap parking area. Descend 0.1 mile through the woods to a T junction at another cement post. Here the Appalachian Trail runs north–south. Turn right (north) onto

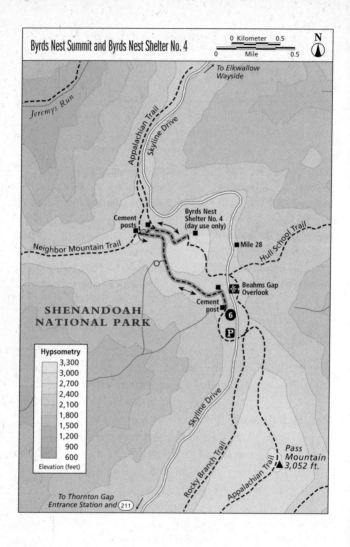

Byrds Nest Summit and Byrds Nest Shelter No. 4

0 Kilometer 0.5
0 Mile 0.5

N

To Elkwallow
Wayside

Jeremys Run

Appalachian Trail

Skyline Drive

Byrds Nest
Shelter No. 4
(day use only)

Cement
posts

Neighbor Mountain Trail

Hull School Trail

Mile 28

Beahms Gap
Overlook

Cement
post

6

P

SHENANDOAH
NATIONAL PARK

Hypsometry

3,300
3,000
2,700
2,400
2,100
1,800
1,500
1,200
900
600

Elevation (feet)

Skyline Drive

Rocky Branch Trail

Appalachian Trail

Pass
Mountain
▲ 3,052 ft.

To Thornton Gap
Entrance Station and (211)

the AT. Soon you'll encounter a cement post indicating a spring on the left.

As you trek through a mostly deciduous forest (pretty in the fall), the trees and rocks offset one another's beauty. There are a few short, steep ascents and a few very rocky areas of trail. Sturdy boots are recommended, especially if the trail is wet.

At 1 mile you'll encounter a four-way junction of the AT and the Neighbor Mountain Trail. Turn right (east) onto the Neighbor Mountain Trail. In 0.1 mile another post is encountered. Here, stay straight on the Neighbor Mountain Trail for 0.5 mile more to Byrds Nest Shelter No. 4.

You'll find the shelter in a pretty setting, one that inspires a picnic. A field lies in front of you, and flowers give color in summer. Pass Mountain rises to the south. If you wander to the right above the shelter, it may be possible to get some views, but nothing outstanding. From here, turn around and retrace your steps to the parking lot.

Miles and Directions

0.0 Cement post, north end of Beahms Gap parking lot.

0.1 Cement post and junction with the Appalachian Trail; turn north (right) onto the AT.

0.5 Spring on left; stay on AT.

1.0 Byrds Nest Summit; four-way cement post at junction with AT and Neighbor Mountain Trail; turn right onto Neighbor Mountain Trail.

1.1 Another cement post; stay straight on Neighbor Mountain Trail.

1.5 Cement post; stay straight on Neighbor Mountain Trail.

1.6 Byrds Nest Shelter No. 4; turn around and retrace your steps.

3.2 Arrive at Beahms Gap parking lot.

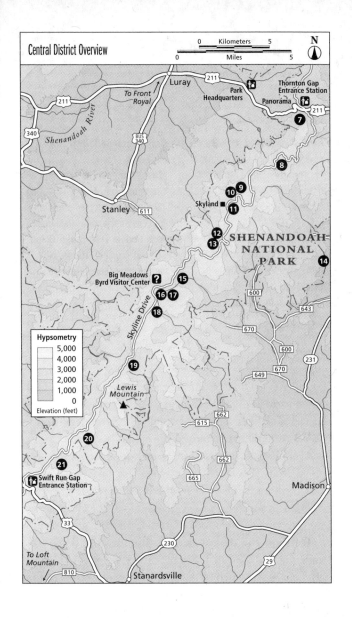

Central District Overview

Kilometers

Miles

N

To Front Royal

Luray

Park Headquarters

Thornton Gap Entrance Station

Panorama

7

8

10 9

Skyland

11

12

13

SHENANDOAH NATIONAL PARK

14

Stanley

Big Meadows Byrd Visitor Center

15

16 17

18

19

Lewis Mountain

Swift Run Gap Entrance Station

20

21

Madison

To Loft Mountain

Stanardsville

Shenandoah River

Hypsometry

5,000
4,000
3,000
2,000
1,000
0

Elevation (feet)

7 Marys Rock North

Appropriate for families, this hike to the summit offers natural history, geology, panoramic views, and folklore.

Start: Skyline Drive Mile 31.6, upper parking lot at Panorama near Thornton Gap Entrance Station
Trailhead GPS: N38 39.549' / W78 19.295'
Type of hike: Out and back
Distance: 3.6 miles
Hiking time: 2 to 4 hours
Difficulty: Easy to moderate
Elevation gain and loss: 1,210 feet

Canine compatibility: Dogs allowed
Maps: National Geographic Trails Illustrated Topo Map 228; *Map 10, Appalachian Trail and Other Trails in Shenandoah National Park, Central District* (PATC, Inc.)
Special considerations: No camping on Marys Rock North Trail.

The Hike

If you have the luxury of time, pick a clear day for this hike and go early in the morning. Sunrise is a great time to enjoy the views and get some superb photos. (Save foggy days for hikes to waterfalls; fog adds to the aura of wetness.)

According to one version of park lore, a young woman named Mary Thornton once made this hike alone to the rocky summit. When she returned she carried a bear cub under each arm. The park certainly does not endorse such intimacy with wildlife today, but the story is a good one.

To begin the trek, walk from the upper parking lot at Panorama and turn left (south) at 0.1 mile onto the Appalachian Trail, which is marked with white blazes. Within

30 yards the trail begins to climb. Twelve log steps help you upward. Within 100 yards five more log steps do the same thing. The trail winds upward through a hardwood forest interspersed with mountain laurel and ferns. It follows the east side of the ridge. Soon the trees are more widely spaced and views begin. The trail becomes very rocky and is fortified on your left with a man-made shelf of rocks. On the upward slope the trees seem to be trying to restrain the force of gravity, preventing large boulders from tumbling down the hillside. The ascent is steady, with some switchbacks and few level areas.

After 1 mile there are large rock monoliths to your right and a lovely panorama to the east. As you approach the summit, the trail swings back into the trees. On the uphill side of the trail, thick stands of mountain laurel line the path. At our approach a ruffed grouse took wing.

At 1.7 miles you will encounter your first cement post. Do not continue on the AT, which veers left. Keep going straight ahead, taking the spur trail to the top, which is 0.1 mile farther. Be sure to follow the blue blazes, not the white ones along the AT.

Marys Rock is composed of Pedlar granodiorite. The vista below is wonderful; you can see Thornton Gap. Plan to spend some time here resting in the clearing or carefully climbing the rocks for different views. You might see peregrine falcons soaring on the wind drafts.

Now that you have climbed 1,210 feet to the top, you can enjoy the luxury of a downhill return. Turn around, retrace your steps to the AT, and go straight (north), but use caution: The steep, rocky descent can be more hazardous than the uphill trek, especially when wet. Follow white blazes back to the Panorama parking lot.

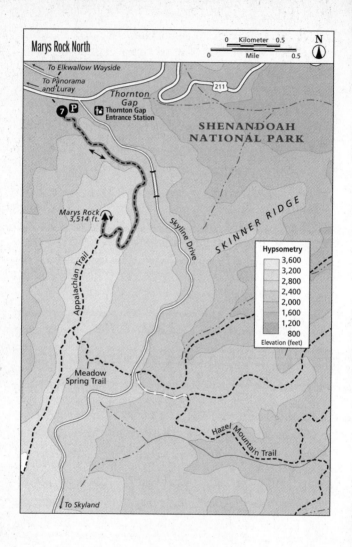

Marys Rock North

To Elkwallow Wayside
To Panorama
and Luray

Thornton
Gap

211

Thornton Gap
Entrance Station

7 P

SHENANDOAH
NATIONAL PARK

Marys Rock
3,514 ft.

SKINNER RIDGE

Appalachian Trail

Skyline Drive

Hypsometry	
	3,600
	3,200
	2,800
	2,400
	2,000
	1,600
	1,200
	800
Elevation (feet)	

Meadow
Spring Trail

Hazel Mountain Trail

To Skyland

0   Kilometer   0.5

0   Mile   0.5

N

Miles and Directions

0.0 Cement post at end of upper parking lot at Panorama.

0.1 Junction with AT; turn left.

1.0 Large rock monoliths on right.

1.7 Cement post; go straight on spur trail; do not turn left on AT.

1.8 Summit of Marys Rock. Retrace your steps to the AT; go straight (north).

3.6 Arrive at upper parking lot at Panorama.

8 Marys Rock South

Appropriate for families, this hike offers natural history, geology, panoramic views, and folklore.

Start: Skyline Drive Mile 33.5, Meadow Spring Trailhead
Trailhead GPS: N38 38.2714' / W78 18.8539'
Type of hike: Out and back
Distance: 2.6 miles
Hiking time: 2 to 3 hours
Difficulty: Moderate
Elevation gain and loss: 830 feet

Canine compatibility: Dogs allowed
Maps: National Geographic Trails Illustrated Topo Map 228; *Map 10, Appalachian Trail and Other Trails in Shenandoah National Park, Central District* (PATC, Inc.)
Special considerations: No camping on Marys Rock South Trail

The Hike

Yet another trail leads to Marys Rock. This route gains less in elevation (830 feet instead of 1,210 feet) and is 0.8 mile shorter, making it an easier alternative to Marys Rock North. Park at Meadow Spring parking on the east side of the road. Walk about 30 feet south along Skyline Drive to access Meadow Spring Trail to Marys Rock. A post reads "No Fires."

The trail begins to ascend immediately, then levels only to climb again. At about 0.4 mile you'll see a huge stone chimney, all that remains of a Potomac Appalachian Trail Club (PATC) hiker cabin. Originally built in the early 1930s, the cabin was torn down in 1939, then rebuilt, only to burn to the ground on Thanksgiving Day of 1946 under mysterious circumstances. From here, the trail ascends. A bench

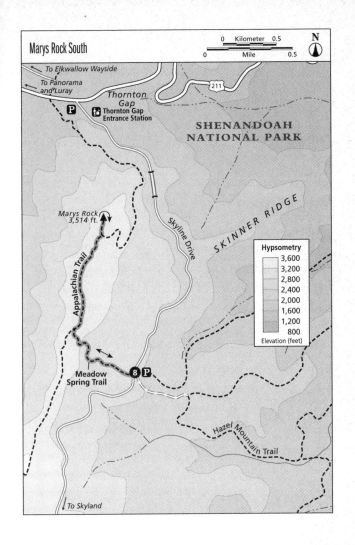

Marys Rock South

To Elkwallow Wayside
To Panorama and Luray

211

Thornton Gap

P

Thornton Gap Entrance Station

SHENANDOAH NATIONAL PARK

Marys Rock 3,514 ft.

SKINNER RIDGE

Appalachian Trail

Skyline Drive

Hypsometry

Elevation (feet)
3,600
3,200
2,800
2,400
2,000
1,600
1,200
800

8 P

Meadow Spring Trail

Hazel Mountain Trail

To Skyland

Kilometer

Mile

provides a nice spot to sit, recoup, and admire the forest of oak, hickory, and maple.

At 0.6 mile you encounter a cement post, and you'll want to turn right here and pick up the AT. The trail ascends, then descends several hundred feet, at which point you come to another post marking another 0.6 mile. Here, you encounter the trail you would have followed if you had begun this hike from Panorama. Turn left onto the spur trail that ascends to Marys Rock summit at 1.3 miles.

Miles and Directions

0.0   Meadow Spring parking lot. Cross Skyline Drive to the west to access the trailhead.

0.6   Cement post at junction with AT; turn right.

1.2   T junction; turn left; follow blue-blazed trail.

1.3   Marys Rock summit; turn around, retrace steps back to trailhead.

2.6   Arrive back at Meadow Spring Trailhead and your car across the Drive.

9 Corbin Cabin Cutoff / Nicholson Hollow / AT Loop

This 5- to 6-hour 4.2-mile hike provides glimpses of the bygone era of the mountain people.

Start: Skyline Drive Mile 37.9, cement post on east side of Skyline Drive
Trailhead GPS: N38 36.9288' / W78 21.0194'
Type of hike: Loop
Distance: 4.3 miles
Hiking time: 3 to 4 hours
Difficulty: Moderately challenging

Elevation gain and loss: 1,095 feet or 1,350 feet
Canine compatibility: Dogs allowed
Maps: National Geographic Trails Illustrated Topo Map 228; *Map 10, Appalachian Trail and Other Trails in Shenandoah National Park, Central District* (PATC, Inc.)

The Hike

On this hike head downhill via the Corbin Cabin Cutoff Trail, ascend via the Nicholson Hollow Trail, and end up on the other side of Skyline Drive by way of the Appalachian Trail. The route passes Freestate Hollow (named by the Nicholson clan) and an abandoned cabin. Visiting a cabin such as this provides a glimpse of what life may have been like for the men, women, and children who once lived in the hollows.

Appropriately, the hike begins by descending a trail built by the mountain people who once inhabited the area. Begin at the Corbin Cabin Cutoff Trailhead on the east side of Skyline Drive and drop gradually for about 25 yards to a cement post that says "Corbin Cabin."

As the steep and rocky trail continues to drop, it is flanked on either side by lush stands of mountain laurel. At about 0.5 mile the trail swings northeast, then abruptly turns to the right (southeast). To your right (west) is a small, dry streambed. Shortly thereafter the trail levels and begins to climb gradually.

At 0.9 mile are the first clear remnants of early human activity. Jumbles of rocks flank the right side of the trail and to the left, downhill, are the ruins of the John R. Nicholson Cabin. The flowing stream below it has a nice pool.

Continue on the trail and rock-hop across the Hughes River to Corbin Cabin. Just before the river, at 1.4 miles, is a cabin that once belonged to Albert and Mamie Nicholson. It is hidden in the trees to the right of the trail. This one is fairly intact, allowing you to get an idea of how it was constructed.

Corbin Cabin is in front of you as you cross the river. The Potomac Appalachian Trail Club (PATC) renovated the cabin in 1954 and now rents it to hikers. The spot is idyllic, and you may want to have a picnic in the yard if no one is currently renting. (**Option:** At this point you may choose to turn around and retrace your steps back to the trailhead, for an out-and-back hike of 2.9 miles, 1.5 to 2 hours.)

To continue on the loop hike, take the old mountain road that leads west from Corbin Cabin. At the junction with Indian Run Trail at 1.6 miles, go straight. This becomes the Nicholson Hollow Trail, which ascends (steeply in places) to Skyline Drive. The first part of the trail is extremely rough and rocky as it crosses Indian Run stream (often dry) at 1.8 miles and climbs through the forest. At 2.9 miles there is a walled-in spring on the left side of the trail, but it is usually dry.

The upper portion of Nicholson Hollow Trail is a fairly straight climb to Skyline Drive. The path is flanked by mountain laurel and oak.

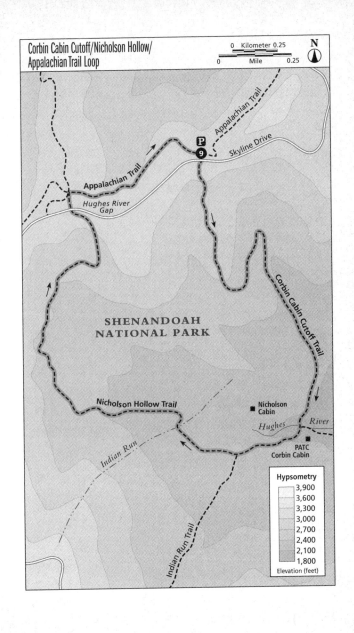

Corbin Cabin Cutoff/Nicholson Hollow/Appalachian Trail Loop

| 0 | Kilometer | 0.25 |
| 0 | Mile | 0.25 |

N

Appalachian Trail

P
9
Skyline Drive

Appalachian Trail

Hughes River Gap

SHENANDOAH
NATIONAL PARK

Corbin Cabin Cutoff Trail

Nicholson Hollow Trail

Nicholson Cabin

Hughes River

Indian Run

PATC Corbin Cabin

Indian Run Trail

Hypsometry

	3,900
	3,600
	3,300
	3,000
	2,700
	2,400
	2,100
	1,800

Elevation (feet)

Upon reaching the Drive at 3.8 miles, turn left and walk south for about 75 yards. Cross the Drive to your right at an opening in the trees and continue straight ahead to access the AT at a cement post. Turn right (north) onto the AT. Follow it as it winds up and down until you reach the parking area, thus completing this scenic loop hike.

Miles and Directions

0.0   Cement post on east side of Skyline Drive at Corbin Cabin Cutoff Trailhead.

0.5   Corbin Cabin Cutoff Trail goes left, then turns abruptly to the right to parallel a streambed.

0.9   Stone wall on right; John R. Nicholson cabin ruins downhill to left.

1.4   Albert and Mamie Nicholson cabin in woods to right of trail.

1.45 Hughes River crossing; cement post below Corbin Cabin (**Option:** turnaround point for out-and-back hike).

1.6   Junction with Indian Run Trail; keep straight on Nicholson Hollow Trail.

1.8   Indian Run stream crossing (often dry).

2.9   Enclosed spring on left.

3.8   Skyline Drive; turn left (south) onto drive; cross drive to cement post; turn right (north) onto AT.

4.3   Arrive at Corbin Cabin Cutoff Trailhead.

10 Stony Man Trail

This is an interpretive trail to the peak of Stony Man Mountain.

Start: Skyline Drive Mile 41.7, cement post just inside Stony Man parking lot at north entrance to Skyland
Trailhead GPS: N38 35.6113' / W78 22.5402'
Type of hike: Out and back
Distance: 1.4 miles
Hiking time: 1 to 2 hours
Difficulty: Easy
Elevation gain and loss: 350 feet
Canine compatibility: Dogs not allowed

Maps: National Geographic Trails Illustrated Topo Map 228; Map 10, *Appalachian Trail and Other Trails in Shenandoah National Park, Central District* (PATC, Inc.)
ROMP Area: On this trail you will approach an area designated as ROMP, an acronym that means Rock Outcrop Management Plan. This is a fragile area—to avoid damage, please do not cross the roped-off area(s).
Special considerations: No camping on the Stony Man Trail.

The Hike

At 4,010 feet, Stony Man is the park's second-highest mountain after Hawksbill. The park provides a brochure (nominal fee) with twenty interpretive site descriptions for this self-guided hike.

From the Stony Man parking area inside Skyland, access the Appalachian Trail at the cement post. Follow the trail right (northeasterly). At 0.4 mile the AT reaches its highest point in Shenandoah. Here, the Stony Man Horse Trail branches off to the left (west) from the AT at a cement post. Go toward the left (north northwest) on the blue-blazed

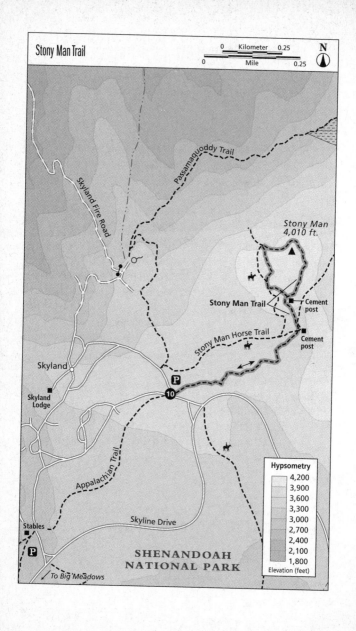

Stony Man Trail

0 Kilometer 0.25
0 Mile 0.25

N

Passamaquoddy Trail

Skyland Fire Road

Stony Man 4,010 ft.

Stony Man Trail

Cement post

Cement post

Stony Man Horse Trail

Skyland

Skyland Lodge

P
10

Appalachian Trail

Skyline Drive

Stables

P

To Big Meadows

SHENANDOAH NATIONAL PARK

Hypsometry

4,200
3,900
3,600
3,300
3,000
2,700
2,400
2,100
1,800

Elevation (feet)

Stony Man Trail. At 0.5 mile the trail splits. Either fork will take you to the summit because the two actually meet to form a loop. At the summit (0.7 mile), take time, particularly in the spring, to search the sky for falcons. Over the years, the National Park Service has sponsored a peregrine falcon re-introduction program intended to restore the nation's fastest diving bird to its wild or native range. Stony Man has served as one of the several release sites.

To complete the hike, continue around the loop, and at the cement post head straight on the AT. You are on familiar ground now. Return to the parking lot the way you came.

Miles and Directions

0.0 From Stony Man parking lot, take the AT north.

0.4 Junction at cement post with Stony Man Horse Trail and Stony Man Trail; go toward the left (north northwest) on blue-blazed Stony Man Trail.

0.5 Fork in trail; either right or left forms loop to viewpoint.

0.7 Summit of Stony Man; complete the loop. At the cement post take Stony Man Trail (blue-blazed) toward the southeast.

1.0 Cement post and junction with AT; head straight south on AT.

1.4 Arrive at Stony Man parking lot.

10A Little Stony Man

Appropriate for families, this hike offers natural history, geology, panoramic views, intimate views of wildflowers

Start: Skyline Drive Mile 35.9, Little Stony Man Trailhead
Trailhead GPS: Little Stony Man Trail: N38 35.5842' / W78 22.5402'
Type of hike: Out and back
Distance: 0.9 mile
Hiking time: About 1 hour
Difficulty: Moderate

Elevation gain and loss: 830 feet
Canine compatibility: Dogs allowed
Maps: National Geographic Trails Illustrated Topo Map 228; *Map 10, Appalachian Trail and Other Trails in Shenandoah National Park, Central District* (PATC, Inc.)

The Hike

Spring is an ideal time to make this 0.9-mile out-and-back hike, particularly if you are interested in seeing the park's floral emblem, the large-flowered trillium (*Trillium grandiflorum*). Typically, this lily blooms from April to May and often comes in both white and purple.

According Ann and Rob Simpson in their book *Wildflowers of Shenandoah National Park*, a nutritious food particle is attached to the seed of the trillium, one that ants carry home. Here, in their mounds, the ants disperse these seeds. In other words, both the seeds and the ants benefit, creating a relationship biologists refer to as symbiosis.

As well as providing a wonderful springtime floral display, the slightly uphill hike to Little Stony Man Cliffs provides sweeping views of Page Valley to the west and of the Skyline Drive to the east. From the Little Stony Man Cliffs, you should also be able to make out the "stony man." Generally, most find his nose first, but that should then help you find his forehead, eye, mouth, and beard.

As you stand at the cliffs, take time to appreciate that the mountains forming your grand setting are some of the oldest mountains on the planet. The volcanic activity that occurred when tectonic plates moved against one another formed these mountains now known as the Appalachians.

You are asked to observe closure and other signs around the rock overlooks, as this is a geologically fragile area.

Miles and Directions

0.0 From Little Stony Man parking lot proceed up the trail.

0.20 Trails splits; continue right.

0.45 Completion of this hike, though a trail to Stony Man continues from this point. Retrace to parking lot.

11 Millers Head

This pretty hike is convenient for the many folks who stay at Skyland during their visit to the park. The short hike starts from the Skyland complex and takes you to an observation platform with delightful views.

Start: Skyline Drive Mile 42.5, south entrance to Skyland; pass stables, take left fork in road, and park at the next gravel road on your left
Trailhead GPS: N38 35.463' / W78 23.039'
Type of hike: Out and back
Distance: 1.6 miles
Hiking time: About 1.5 hours

Difficulty: Easy
Elevation gain and loss: 475 feet
Canine compatibility: Dogs allowed
Maps: National Geographic Trails Illustrated Topo Map 228; *Map 10, Appalachian Trail and Other Trails in Shenandoah National Park, Central District* (PATC, Inc.)

The Hike

From the trailhead, begin your hike by walking up the gravel road from your car to the cement post at Millers Head Trail. This will take you to the summit of Bushytop Mountain at 0.2 mile. There you will see some large microwave dishes, part of the Skyland communication system.

Once on Millers Head Trail, head downhill via a series of switchbacks. About 0.5 mile before the observation platform, there is a cement post. Keep going down the trail to the platform. Along the way there are some good views, but none are as nice as the one from the Millers Head observation platform at 0.8 mile, at an elevation of about 3,460 feet. From here you can get full views of the Page Valley, the town

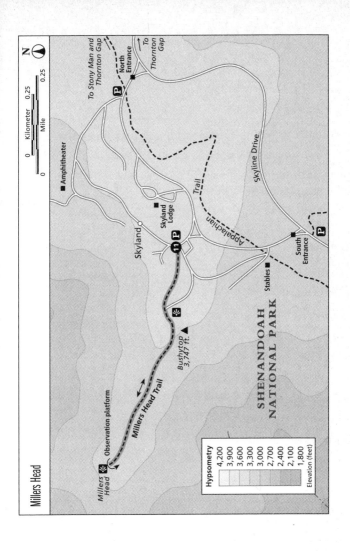

Millers Head

of Luray, Massanutten Mountain, Stony Man, Hawksbill, and Marys and Bettys Rocks. Turn around and retrace your steps to the trailhead.

Miles and Directions

0.0 Trailhead at cement post, 75 yards uphill from parking area.

0.2 Summit of Bushytop; begin descent on Millers Head Trail.

0.5 Cement post; head downhill to observation platform.

0.8 Observation platform on Millers Head; turn around and retrace steps.

1.6 Arrive back at trailhead.

12 Limberlost

Enjoy a short walk along a crushed greenstone surface.

Start: Skyline Drive Mile 43.0, turn east at the Limberlost Trail sign and park in the Limberlost parking lot
Trailhead GPS: N38 34.830' / W78 22.777'
Type of hike: Loop
Distance: 1.3 miles
Hiking time: About 1 hour
Difficulty: Easy

Elevation gain and loss: 100 feet
Canine compatibility: Dogs not allowed
Maps: National Geographic Trails Illustrated Topo Map 228; *Map 10, Appalachian Trail and Other Trails in Shenandoah National Park, Central District* (PATC, Inc.)

The Hike

The Limberlost Trail, once lined by ancient hemlocks, can provide inspiration for all.

Addie Pollock laid the groundwork for preserving the Limberlost Forest. Around 1920 she bought one hundred of the largest trees in the area for $1,000. Her husband George, who established Skyland, named the remnant forest after the Gene Stratton-Porter novel *A Girl of the Limberlost*, though in that case "limberlost" referred to a fictitious setting in Indiana.

Here in Shenandoah, the Limberlost Forest also preserves some of the park's oldest and largest red spruce trees. This species is a remnant from the last ice age, and one such tree is believed to be more than 250 years old. This patriarch stands alone by a small stream that you will encounter along the walk.

Because the Limberlost has been designated an Outstanding Natural Area, no bicycles, pets, or camping are allowed along the trail. The trail was officially dedicated in the summer of 1997.

After parking, read the information on the trailhead sign and the cement post. Note that other trails radiate from and cross the Limberlost Trail.

The nearly level path is lined with mountain laurel. Until recently, it was also rimmed by ancient hemlock trees, some said to be 400 years old. Sadly, the exotic insect pest known as the woolly adelgid, which sucks the stored food from the hemlock needles, has wreaked havoc on Limberlost's hemlocks. Now most are gone, having either fallen or been cut down for safety. The trees will lie in place, gradually decaying into the soil. A different plant life-form will begin to arise now that the sun can reach the forest floor.

The oak trees in Limberlost have also suffered greatly due to gypsy moth invasions. However, wildflowers bloom in spring and summer; and white pine, birch, and maple trees still flourish in this beautiful place. Limberlost encompasses the story of a changing forest.

As you meander through what was once an old meadow, notice the abundance of wood benches for resting and observing. There is a bench about every 400 feet. Cross a boardwalk over a wet, swampy area; at 0.4 mile a cement post indicates that Crescent Rock Trail enters the Limberlost Trail from the right (south) at Skyline Drive. Stay on Limberlost Trail, which proceeds straight ahead and offers yet another lesson in the devastating power of nature. In the fall of 1996, Tropical Storm Fran swept through the area, uprooting many mature trees and causing extensive trail erosion, which was repaired in 1997 after several months of work.

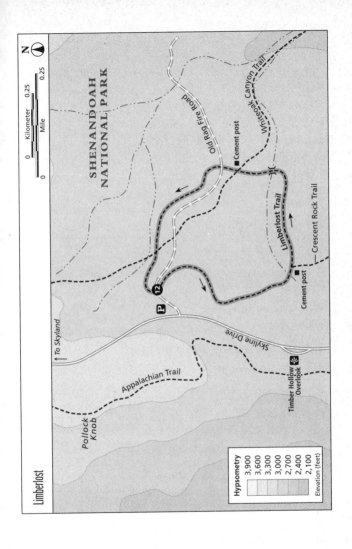

Limberlost

SHENANDOAH
NATIONAL PARK

N

0   Kilometer   0.25

0   Mile   0.25

To Skyland

Pollock
Knob

Appalachian Trail

P

12

Old Rag Fire Road

Cement post

Whiteoak Canyon Trail

Limberlost Trail

Crescent Rock Trail

Cement post

Skyline Drive

Timber Hollow
Overlook

Hypsometry

3,900
3,600
3,300
3,000
2,700
2,400
2,100

Elevation (feet)

At 0.7 mile cross a large wooden bridge. Another cement post points the way to the Whiteoak Canyon Trail access.

At 0.8 mile another cement post shows the Whiteoak Canyon Trail going left and right. On your right you will confront an interesting rock extrusion known as "Rock of Ages." The monolith is an outstanding example of columnar jointing and exists because of an ancient lava flow that now juts from the earth like a giant crystal. Stay on the crushed-greenstone trail with the Limberlost markers to trail's end and back to the parking lot.

Miles and Directions

0.0 Trailhead 50 yards from Skyline Drive.

0.4 Cement post; junction with Crescent Rock Trail; stay on Limberlost Trail.

0.7 Cross wooden bridge.

0.8 Intersection of Whiteoak Canyon Trail; stay on Limberlost Trail.

1.2 Cross the Whiteoak Canyon Trail again.

1.3 Arrive at trailhead.

13 Hawksbill Summit

This loop hike to the summit of the park's highest mountain offers spectacular views.

Start: Skyline Drive Mile 45.6, Hawksbill Gap parking area; access trailhead at north end of lot
Trailhead GPS: N38 33.39' / W78 23.17'
Type of hike: Loop
Distance: 2.8 miles
Hiking time: 2 to 3 hours
Difficulty: Moderate
Elevation gain and loss: About 800 feet
Canine compatibility: Dogs allowed

Maps: National Geographic Trails Illustrated Topo Map 228; *Map 10, Appalachian Trail and Other Trails in Shenandoah National Park, Central District* (PATC, Inc.)
ROMP Area: On this trail you will approach an area designated as ROMP, an acronym that means Rock Outcrop Management Plan. This is a fragile area—to avoid damage, please do not cross the roped-off area(s).
Special considerations: No camping on Hawksbill Mountain.

The Hike

The trail begins at the north end of Hawksbill Gap parking lot. A level spur trail about 100 yards long leads to the Appalachian Trail, which is marked with white blazes. Turn left (south) onto the AT and begin climbing. The trail is rocky, and as always, good hiking boots are recommended. At 0.4 mile the trail approaches a talus slope (scattered rock). After another 25 yards it passes a second talus slope, and there is a view of mountains and valleys spilling off to the west. A half mile from the trailhead, the trail approaches yet another rock-strewn outcropping, suggestive once again of the erosion of the park's mountains. Lichen cover the rocks, and here and there trees struggle for a foothold in soils that were formed relatively recently.

Toward the summit, foxtail blooms in great abundance; columbine also appears, as does a species of wild geranium. Several rock outcrops tilt upward, revealing layers that look like a stack of pancakes. The area is one of outstanding natural splendor.

At 1 mile you will come to a cement post noting the mileage along the AT and the distance to Rock Spring Cabin. The post points toward Hawksbill and back toward Fishers Gap. Make a hard left turn onto the Salamander Trail at this point and continue climbing. Within 0.25 mile of the junction, the rocks covering the trail become more exposed, probably the result of tremendous spring runoff. Near the top, the trail joins a fire road. Keep climbing to the summit, which is not far away, at 1.9 miles. At the summit there is a shelter named Byrds Nest. The three-sided structure was built with funds provided by former U.S. senator and Virginia governor Harry F. Byrd Sr.; it is one of four such shelters in the park. No water is available at the site, and camping is not permitted on or near the summit.

The shelter is surrounded by red spruce, balsam fir, and mountain ash. Continue the last few yards to the observation platform and the highest point in the park.

At 4,051 feet, Hawksbill is the park's highest peak, making it an ideal place for birds. The endangered peregrine falcon (*Falco peregrinus*) has been recorded at Hawksbill and several other surrounding mountains. Peregrines are the nation's swiftest avian species, capable of diving at speeds up to 120 miles per hour.

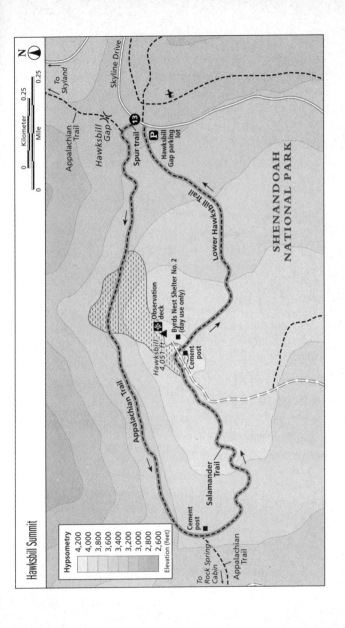

Hawksbill Summit

Hypsometry
4,200
4,000
3,800
3,600
3,400
3,200
3,000
2,800
2,600
Elevation (feet)

N

0   0.25
Kilometer

0   0.25
Mile

To
Skyline

Appalachian
Trail

Hawksbill Gap

Spur trail

13

P   Hawksbill
         Gap parking
         lot

Lower Hawksbill Trail

Skyline Drive

SHENANDOAH
NATIONAL PARK

Appalachian Trail

Hawksbill
4,051 ft.

Observation
deck

Byrds Nest Shelter No. 2
(day use only)

Cement
post

Salamander
Trail

Cement
post

To
Rock Spring
Cabin

Appalachian
Trail

The view from the top of Hawksbill is commanding and panoramic. Mountains roll off in all directions, blending gradually into yet more mountains in the hazy distance. The Park Service has placed a huge compass at the overlook to help those with maps orient themselves. Stony Man, with its jagged features, is to the north; Browns Mountain spreads neatly to the west. To the south is Graves Mountain. Just below, Skyline Drive threads through the hardwood forest. The town of Luray is to the northwest.

To return to Hawksbill Gap parking lot from the summit, retrace your steps to the shelter and go left on the fire road to a cement post that marks Lower Hawksbill Trail. Turn left and follow the trail back to the parking lot. ***Note:*** The descent is steep and the going a bit slow for some.

Miles and Directions

0.0 Trailhead at Hawksbill Gap parking lot; access AT at the end of a 100-yard spur trail; turn left (west).

0.4 First of three talus slopes, some views.

1.0 Cement post; make hard left onto Salamander Trail.

1.9 Hawksbill summit and observation deck.

2.1 Cement post below and left of shelter, turn left onto Lower Hawksbill Trail.

2.8 Arrive at trailhead at Hawksbill Gap parking lot.

14 Whiteoak Canyon

This hike travels to some of the park's most spectacular waterfalls.

Start: Skyline Drive Mile 31.5 (Thornton Gap); take US 211 east to Sperryville; continue to US 522 south; go 0.8 mile, turn right onto VA 231, and go about 9.5 miles to SR 643; south on SR 643 for about 10 miles to junction with SR 600; turn right (west) onto SR 600 and stay on this road for 3.6 miles, to the point where the road fords Cedar Run. You will see the parking lot from here. The trailhead is at the far end.
Trailhead GPS: N38 32.329' / W78 20.890'

Type of hike: Out and back
Distance: 5.8 miles
Hiking time: About 3 hours
Difficulty: Moderate to most challenging
Elevation gain and loss: About 1,670 feet
Canine compatibility: Dogs allowed
Maps: National Geographic Trails Illustrated Topo Map 228; *Map 10, Appalachian Trail and Other Trails in Shenandoah National Park, Central District* (PATC, Inc.)

The Hike

Although this hike is almost 6 miles long, we have included it here because there is so much to see along the way. The inbound portion of the hike is uphill, but at any time you can turn around and make the easy downhill hike back to the trailhead.

This hike provides access to some of the most spectacular falls in the park. The farther you go, the more falls you will pass—six if you complete the entire hike.

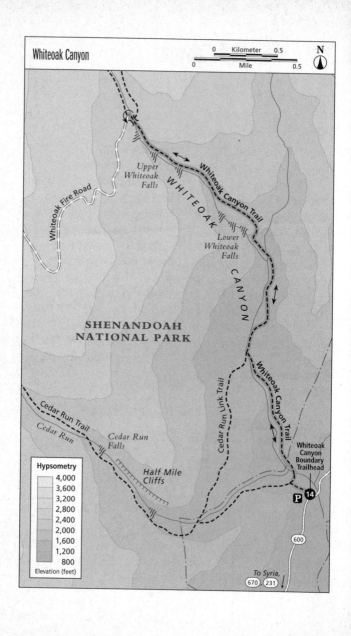

Whiteoak Canyon

Kilometer 0.5
Mile 0.5

N

Upper Whiteoak Falls

Whiteoak Fire Road

WHITEOAK

Whiteoak Canyon Trail

Lower Whiteoak Falls

CANYON

SHENANDOAH NATIONAL PARK

Cedar Run Trail

Cedar Run

Cedar Run Falls

Half Mile Cliffs

Cedar Run Link Trail

Whiteoak Canyon Trail

Whiteoak Canyon Boundary Trailhead

P 14

600

To Syria, 670 231

Hypsometry

4,000
3,600
3,200
2,800
2,400
2,000
1,600
1,200
800

Elevation (feet)

Begin your hike from the parking lot just off SR 600 and follow the Whiteoak Canyon Trail, which crosses Cedar Run almost immediately via a footbridge. At 0.1 mile a cement post indicates the junction with Cedar Run Trail from the left. Stay right on Whiteoak Canyon Trail. At 0.7 mile continue to your right on the Whiteoak Canyon Trail. This is the junction with Cedar Run Link Trail, which leads to a part of Shenandoah that has been designated as wilderness.

The ascent of Whiteoak Canyon is steep and may require scrambling around numerous rocks. That is the bad news. The good news is that at 1.5 miles, a cement post marks the base of the first falls, and the trail swings to the right. At 1.8 miles there are great views of waterfalls and pools. If you take your time, stopping to snack, eat lunch, or dangle your feet in the water, you should be able to make it to a spur trail at 2.7 miles, which leads you to the base of Whiteoak Falls overlook without too much effort.

The last falls are at 2.9 miles. The point is marked by a cement post. Simply turn around here and enjoy the views again as you make your way downhill and back to the parking lot.

Miles and Directions

0.0 From the parking lot, cross a footbridge and proceed along Whiteoak Canyon Trail.

0.1 Cement post designates intersection with Cedar Run Trail; stay right on Whiteoak Canyon Trail.

0.7 Cedar Run Link Trail comes in from the left; stay right on Whiteoak Canyon Trail.

1.5 Cement post at base of first falls; trail swings to the right.

1.8 View of falls and pool from the rocks to the left of the trail.

2.7 Spur trail leads 0.1 mile to base of Whiteoak Falls.

2.9 Whiteoak Falls overlook on left; turn around, retrace steps.

5.8 Arrive at parking lot.

15 Dark Hollow Falls

This is a short out-and-back hike to one of the park's most popular and easily accessible waterfalls.

Start: Skyline Drive Mile 50.7
Trailhead GPS: N38 31.105' / W78 25.512'
Type of hike: Out and back
Distance: 1.4 miles
Hiking time: 1.5 to 2 hours
Difficulty: Challenging on return
Elevation gain and loss: 440 feet

Canine compatibility: Dogs not allowed
Maps: National Geographic Trails Illustrated Topo Map 228; *Map 10, Appalachian Trail and Other Trails in Shenandoah National Park, Central District* (PATC, Inc.)

The Hike

The trail descends from the parking lot and follows Hogcamp Branch. At 0.6 mile there is an overlook of 70-foot Dark Hollow Falls. (***Note:*** The rails along the trail should not require a statement of intent but apparently do; invariably, some visitors fail to realize that the fences are intended not only to prevent further erosion but also to save life and limb. This is one place with a history of injury. Please remain on the trail! Rocks can be wet and very slippery.)

Continue to the base of Dark Hollow Falls at 0.7 mile. If you enjoy the spectacle, be aware that you are in good company. According to a resident naturalist, Thomas Jefferson also once appreciated this scene.

The falls are obviously appealing, especially if you consider their source. Hogcamp Branch drains the Big Meadow Swamp, which can be relatively dry during some of the summer. Nevertheless, Hogcamp manages to gather enough

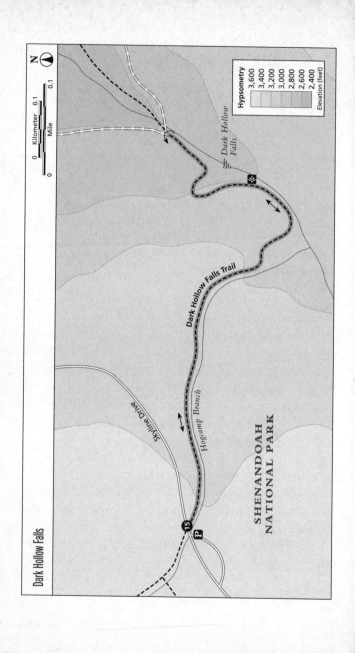

Dark Hollow Falls

Hypsometry

Elevation (feet)
3,600
3,400
3,200
3,000
2,800
2,600
2,400

N

0   Kilometer   0.1

0   Mile   0.1

Dark Hollow Falls Trail

Dark Hollow Falls

Skyline Drive

Hogcamp Branch

15

P

SHENANDOAH
NATIONAL PARK

water in its progression toward Dark Hollow Falls to create a lovely scene. From here, turn around and return to the trailhead; or you can descend farther to enjoy yet other falls created by Hogcamp Branch. From the base of Dark Hollow Falls, climb about 440 feet in elevation back to your starting point. The descent to the falls is the easy part of the hike (unless you have tricky knees), so remember: In Shenandoah, what goes down generally has to come back up.

Miles and Directions

0.0   Parking lot.

0.6   Overlook of Dark Hollow Falls.

0.7   Base of Dark Hollow Falls; retrace your steps.

1.4   Arrive at parking lot.

16 Story of the Forest Trail

This easy, 1- to 2-hour interpretive round-trip hike follows a trail that shows plant succession in the surrounding Blue Ridge forest.

Start: Skyline Drive Mile 51.0. At the Byrd Visitor Center, take a right in the parking lot, cross the road to the trailhead, which is immediately in front.
Trailhead GPS: N38 31.141' / W78 26.180'
Type of hike: Loop
Distance: 1.8 miles
Hiking time: 1 to 2 hours

Difficulty: Easy
Elevation gain and loss: 290 feet
Canine compatibility: Dogs not allowed
Maps: National Geographic Trails Illustrated Topo Map 228; *Map 10, Appalachian Trail and Other Trails in Shenandoah National Park, Central District* (PATC, Inc.)

The Hike

This delightful, informative walk is a self-guided tour to the wonders of a Blue Ridge forest. It's a hike for everyone, especially children, as they will probably get good views of wildlife.

At the trailhead bear right (the maintenance area is to the left). You will be on a wide trail, which is gravel, forest floor, then paved. At 0.2 mile cross a bridge over Hog Branch and stay left. Then keep straight at the junction with a horse trail at 0.4 mile.

When you reach the Big Meadows Campground at 0.8 mile, turn left and follow the paved biking and walking path leading back to the visitor center and trailhead.

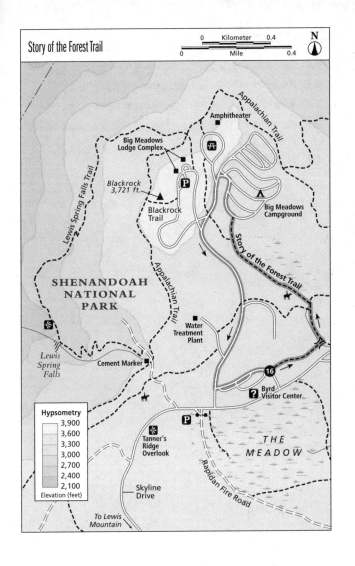

Miles and Directions

0.0   Trailhead; stay on paved path to the right.

0.2   Bridge over Hogcamp Branch; stay left at junction.

0.4   Junction with horse trail; keep going straight.

0.8   Big Meadows Campground; turn left to access paved biking/
walking path.

1.8   Arrive at trailhead.

17 Lewis Spring Falls

This easy, 1- to 2-hour interpretive round-trip hike follows a trail that again dramatizes plant succession in the surrounding Blue Ridge forest.

Start: Skyline Drive Mile 51.2, Big Meadows Campground
Trailhead GPS: N38 31.523' / W78 26.253'
Type of hike: Loop
Distance: 3.3 miles
Hiking time: 3 to 4 hours
Difficulty: Moderate to challenging because of rocks
Elevation gain and loss: 990 feet
Canine compatibility: Dogs allowed
Maps: National Geographic Trails Illustrated Topo Map 228; *Map 10, Appalachian Trail and Other Trails in Shenandoah National Park, Central District* (PATC, Inc.)

Special considerations: Be sure to carry water on this hike. Signs caution hikers not to drink the water found along the way. Some water is contaminated and requires vigorous boiling. One common contaminant is giardia, a waterborne parasite that can cause severe diarrhea, cramps, and fatigue. The parasite can survive in very cold water and is spread by the droppings of dogs, horses, cattle, elk, rabbits, and other small mammals, as well as humans.

The Hike

Walk to the amphitheater behind the picnic area. Take the Appalachian Trail south (left). Below the amphitheater, at the cement post, pick up the blue blazes of the Lewis Spring Falls Trail, which branches to the right at 0.1 mile. (*Note:* If you want to stay on the AT, Milam Gap is 2.6 miles south; Fishers Gap is 1.6 miles north.)

This well-maintained trail descends immediately and continues to do so for about a mile. The rocky trail requires sturdy hiking boots. (*Caution:* Watch yourself on the rocks—even dry ones can be slippery.) Notice the many fallen trees, evidence of the power of ice and wind storms.

The path is flanked on both sides by hardwood trees and low-growth bushes. Descend into a hollow with some granite outcroppings. *Note:* Stay alert for wildlife. Deer abound, and on our hike we ran into a member of a less-welcome species—one of the forest's spotted skunks, a unique member of the weasel family. Though the animal lifted its tail, it also lowered it as we backed off, so we carried no bad smell back to our tent.

When the trail finally levels, you can hear the falls; at 1 mile another brief ascent brings you to a nice overlook with views to the western mountains. Turn left, to the southeast, and follow the blue blazes to the observation point. Cross a small stream and parallel an iron railing. *Caution:* Do not attempt to climb down to the base of the falls. People have suffered serious, even fatal, injuries trying this.

Lewis Spring Falls is the fourth-highest falls in the park. It's a beautiful, gentle falls that cascades 81 feet. At 1.3 miles you can get a safe and commanding view of the falls from an observation point that was constructed by young men working in the Civilian Conservation Corps (CCC) camps in the 1930s.

From the overlook, backtrack north for about 50 feet and pick up the blue blazes going east. The trail maintains an uphill grade, sure and steady. It parallels a creek on your right and then switchbacks away from the stream.

After a climb there is a cement marker at 1.9 miles. Go east for 70 yards on Lewis Spring Fire Road, then turn left

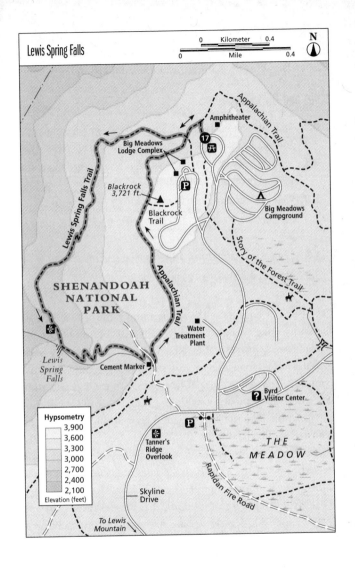

Lewis Spring Falls

Kilometer 0 — 0.4
Mile 0 — 0.4

N

Amphitheater

Appalachian Trail

17

Big Meadows
Lodge Complex

P

Blackrock
3,721 ft.

Blackrock
Trail

Big Meadows
Campground

Story of the Forest Trail

Lewis Spring Falls Trail

SHENANDOAH
NATIONAL
PARK

Appalachian Trail

Water
Treatment
Plant

Lewis
Spring
Falls

Cement Marker

Byrd
Visitor Center

Hypsometry
3,900
3,600
3,300
3,000
2,700
2,400
2,100
Elevation (feet)

Tanner's
Ridge
Overlook

P

THE
MEADOW

Skyline
Drive

Rapidan Fire Road

To Lewis
Mountain

(north) onto the AT. Follow the white blazes on the trees. From this point (you are still chugging uphill), follow the trail to Big Meadows Lodge and the campground.

Miles and Directions

0.0 Amphitheater behind picnic area at Big Meadows Campground; access AT to the left, just off paved road.

0.1 Junction; take Lewis Spring Falls Trail (blue blazes) and begin descent (west and south).

1.0 View to west; turn south to overlook.

1.3 Falls observation point, 250 feet ahead; backtrack to main trail.

1.9 Cement marker; go east 70 yards to access AT.

3.3 Arrive at Big Meadows campground.

Option: For families with children under the age of 9 or 10, the above hike to Lewis Spring Falls may be too strenuous. A somewhat shorter, easier alternative is to descend a wide gravel service road that is just south of the Big Meadows complex. Pass yellow-blazed horse trails to the left and right and come to a junction with the AT at 0.3 mile. Just past the junction, take the blue-blazed Lewis Spring Falls Trail on your left. Follow that for 0.6 mile to another junction. Here, take the spur trail to your left, which leads to a nice overlook near the top of the falls. Retrace your steps from this point, which will be mostly uphill.

This hike is 2 miles long and has an elevation gain and loss of about 800 feet. If you are hiking with young children, this may take 2 to 3 hours. Be sure to carry sufficient water.

18 Rapidan Camp

This is a moderately difficult hike to a falls, the retreat of a former U.S. president, and a return along one of the park's higher and more geologically interesting peaks.

Start: Skyline Drive Mile 52.8, parking lot at Milam Gap; access the Appalachian Trail on the other side of Skyline Drive
Trailhead GPS: N38 29.530' / W78 26.446'
Type of hike: Out and back
Distance: 4.0 miles
Hiking time: 2 to 3 hours
Difficulty: Moderate

Elevation gain and loss: About 850 feet
Canine compatibility: Dogs allowed
Maps: National Geographic Trails Illustrated Topo Map 228; *Map 10, Appalachian Trail and Other Trails in Shenandoah National Park, Central District* (PATC, Inc.)

The Hike

To reach the trailhead, cross Skyline Drive to the side opposite the parking lot. From here, follow the AT for a short distance until you reach its junction with Mill Prong Trail. Turn left (eastward) onto Mill Prong Trail and begin a gradual descent, paralleling Mill Prong. A sign explains that "Fishing Is Permitted" in the stream. However, it also says "All fish must be handled carefully and returned immediately to the stream" and "Only artificial flies or lures with a single hook are permitted."

After 1.5 miles the trail passes Big Rock Falls. Continue following the trail downhill, until you encounter a bridge crossing Mill Prong, which is almost immediately adjacent

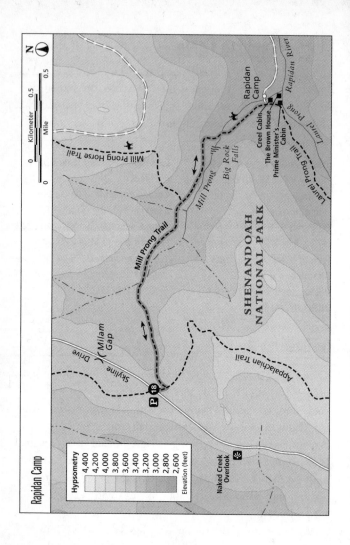

Rapidan Camp

Hypsometry

4,400
4,200
4,000
3,800
3,600
3,400
3,200
3,000
2,800
2,600
Elevation (feet)

Naked Creek Overlook

Skyline Drive

Milam Gap

P 18

Mill Prong Trail

Mill Prong

Big Rock Falls

Mill Prong Horse Trail

Appalachian Trail

SHENANDOAH NATIONAL PARK

Creel Cabin
The Brown House
Prime Minister's Cabin

Rapidan Camp

Laurel Prong Trail

Laurel Prong

Rapidan River

N

0   0.5   Kilometer
0   0.5   Mile

to the Rapidan River. At 2 miles cross the bridge and climb the short bank to Rapidan Camp.

President Herbert Hoover came to Rapidan Camp (formerly called Camp Hoover in his honor) for rest and relaxation. He was an avid outdoorsman and enjoyed fishing the many nearby creeks. Thirteen structures provided the backdrop for his vacations, which were often working vacations. Of the original thirteen, only three remain: the Brown House (which has been fully restored, inside and out), the Creel Cabin, and the Prime Minister's Cabin. The setting is just as beautiful today as it was when Hoover retreated to Shenandoah. To him, the retreat met three key criteria: It was within 100 miles of Washington, DC; it was located on a trout stream; and it was 2,500 feet above sea level. Because of the historic significance of the area, Congress has designated Rapidan Camp a historic landmark.

Laurel Prong and Mill Prong converge near the camp to create the Rapidan River. The river is full of deep pools that still contain trout like those that enticed President Hoover. After visiting these historic structures, turn around and retrace your steps to the Milam Gap parking lot.

Miles and Directions

0.0 Milam Gap parking lot; go about 40 yards on the AT; turn left onto Mill Prong Trail.

0.7 Cross stream.

1.1 Cross stream.

1.5 Big Rock Falls.

2.0 Rapidan Camp; turn around, retrace steps.

4.0 Arrive at Milam Gap parking lot.

19 Bearfence Mountain

This short hike offers a 360-degree view and a real rock scramble toward the summit.

Start: Skyline Drive Mile 56.4, Bearfence Mountain parking lot; access Bearfence Mountain Trail at cement post on other side of Skyline Drive
Trailhead GPS: N38 27.0857' / W78 28.0109'
Type of hike: Loop
Distance: 1.2 miles
Hiking time: 1 to 2 hours

Difficulty: Moderate
Elevation gain and loss: 380 feet
Canine compatibility: Dogs not allowed
Maps: National Geographic Trails Illustrated Topo Map 228; *Map 10, Appalachian Trail and Other Trails in Shenandoah National Park, Central District* (PATC, Inc.)

The Hike

Bearfence Mountain (3,640 feet) is one of several summits in the park that command a complete panoramic view: Massanutten Mountain and the Shenandoah Valley to the west and Laurel Gap, Fork Mountain, and Bluff Mountain to the east. In the short hike from the parking lot to the summit, you pass through the sandstone of the Swift Run Formation, capped by Catoctin basalt.

Hiking to the summit requires some degree of coordination. Though expertise in rock climbing is not necessary, you'll need some dexterity to maneuver through jumbled rocks. In some cases you may find yourself scooting along on your bottom. To ensure good traction and to diminish the possibility of bruised feet, we recommend that you wear good hiking boots, although they won't help much if the rocks are wet or covered with snow. In summer park officials have seen rattlesnakes in the area, so watch where you place your feet and hands. Park handouts indicate that this is not a trail for small children, especially those who must be carried.

Almost immediately after leaving the parking lot, the blue-blazed trail climbs uphill, and at 0.1 mile it crosses the Appalachian Trail. In several places there are trees felled by the many severe storms that have taken place since 1996. Their giant, exposed roots provide mute testimony to the humbling power of nature.

Within 300 yards of the parking lot, the trail begins to thread through huge boulders. This rock was originally volcanic lava, but with millions of years of compression, it has metamorphosed into the gray-green rock you see today. Appropriately, it is called greenstone, but only recent fractures reveal the green coloration.

If you are out of shape, it may seem as though the tortuous maze of boulders will never end, but the trail opens within a few hundred yards. At 0.4 mile you know you have reached the Bearfence summit when you can peer down on everything. Looking east, you can see mountains ranging from Hazeltop to Kirtley. Looking west, you can see Skyline Drive, the Shenandoah Valley, and Devils Tanyard. You are standing 3,640 feet above sea level.

To continue toward the AT, turn right (west) from the summit. Intersect with the AT at the cement post, 0.5 mile, and take the trail north. Return to the parking lot. (**Option:** From Bearfence Mountain, you can retrace your steps to the parking lot for a total hike of 0.8 mile.)

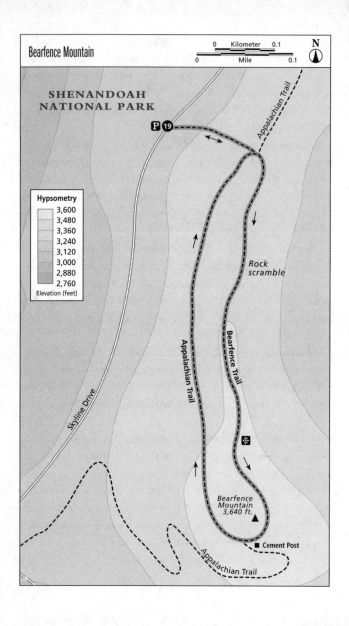

Bearfence Mountain

SHENANDOAH
NATIONAL PARK

P 19

Appalachian Trail

Hypsometry

3,600
3,480
3,360
3,240
3,120
3,000
2,880
2,760
Elevation (feet)

Rock
scramble

Appalachian Trail

Bearfence Trail

Skyline Drive

Bearfence
Mountain
3,640 ft.

Cement Post

Appalachian Trail

0   Kilometer   0.1
0   Mile   0.1

N

Miles and Directions

0.0 Bearfence Mountain parking lot; cement post, east side of Skyline Drive; trail ascends (blue blazes).

0.1 Cross AT.

0.4 Bearfence summit; continue west toward AT.

0.5 AT junction; turn right and descend on AT.

0.6 Close loop; turn left (west toward parking lot).

1.2 Arrive at Bearfence Mountain parking lot.

20 Pocosin Trail

This inspiring venture along an easy trail provides insights into Shenandoah's history and wildlife.

Start: Skyline Drive Mile 59.5, trail begins 50 yards down Pocosin Fire Road
Trailhead GPS: N38 24.433' / W78 28.964'
Type of hike: Out and back
Distance: 2.0 miles
Hiking time: 1 to 2 hours
Difficulty: Easy

Elevation gain and loss: 450 feet
Canine compatibility: Dogs allowed
Maps: National Geographic Trails Illustrated Topo Map 228; *Map 10, Appalachian Trail and Other Trails in Shenandoah National Park, Central District* (PATC, Inc.)

The Hike

Locate the trailhead by driving to Mile 59.5 on Skyline Drive. Turn onto Pocosin Fire Trail on the east side of the drive. Park near the yellow chain and begin your hike down the fire road, which proceeds in an easterly direction and crosses the Appalachian Trail at 0.1 mile. At the cement post at 0.2 mile, stay on the fire road as it approaches the Pocosin Cabin, one in a chain of Potomac Appalachian Trail Club (PATC) cabins that serve hikers using the AT. Managed by the PATC, they are available for rent. To visit the cabin (if unoccupied), turn right onto the side path.

Continue along the fire trail, which begins a slight descent. Throughout the spring and summer—and sometimes into the fall—wildflowers flank the trail. Look for columbine in the late spring and milkweed in the summer. The latter is associated with disturbed sites.

Soon the trail levels, and at 0.9 mile you encounter a cement post on the right that indicates the Pocosin Horse Trail (yellow blazes). As you pass the horse trail, look immediately to the right at what seems to be an old mountain cabin. This is actually part of the ruins of an Episcopal mission established here around 1904. Near the ruined cabin is all that remains of the old church—its stone steps.

Explore and let your imagination run loose. Story has it that in 1904 a young minister wanted to build an Episcopal mission in the dark, brooding hollow the locals then called the "Dark Pocosan." The locals violently opposed the mission, but rather than let that scare him off, the minister approached a local mountain man and said, "I hear you want to kill me." The mountain man was so impressed with the minister's bravery that the minister was able to build the new mission without incident. The church soon attracted residents of the Dark Pocosan (later Pocosin), who came to worship driving horse-drawn carriages and sometimes hiking the paths.

Though the forest is swallowing the artifacts of the period, a number of features from the mission days still remain. Old stone stairs and crumbling mission walls are among them. *Caution:* Hiking the several trails that take you to the old mission provides a rewarding excursion, but remember that old timbers and dilapidated rock walls attract snakes, so watch where you are going and where you put your hands.

Once you have finished exploring, turn around and retrace your steps to the trailhead.

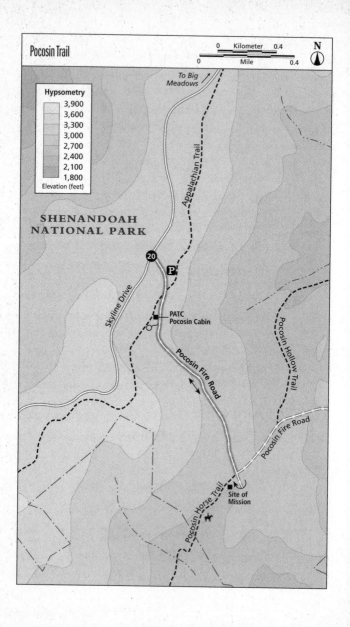

Pocosin Trail

Hypsometry

3,900
3,600
3,300
3,000
2,700
2,400
2,100
1,800
Elevation (feet)

SHENANDOAH
NATIONAL PARK

To Big
Meadows

Appalachian Trail

Skyline Drive

20

P

PATC
Pocosin Cabin

Pocosin Fire Road

Pocosin Hollow Trail

Pocosin Fire Road

Pocosin Horse Trail

Site of
Mission

N

0   Kilometer   0.4
0   Mile   0.4

Miles and Directions

0.0 Trailhead; pass chain and follow yellow-blazed Pocosin Fire Trail.

0.1 Cement post; stay on fire trail; cross AT.

0.2 Cement post; stay on fire trail; PATC Pocosin Cabin (locked) to right.

0.9 Cement post on right; junction with Pocosin Horse Trail and Pocosin Fire Road / Hollow Trail to left; continue just past horse trail.

1.0 Ruins of Episcopal mission on right; turn around, retrace steps.

2.0 Arrive trailhead.

21 South River Falls

This enjoyable hike leads to the park's third-highest waterfall.

Start: Skyline Drive Mile 62.8, South River picnic area
Trailhead GPS: N38 22.8901' / W78 31.0064'
Type of hike: Out and back
Distance: 4.4 miles
Hiking time: 2 to 3 hours
Difficulty: Moderate

Elevation gain and loss: 800 feet
Canine compatibility: Dogs allowed
Maps: National Geographic Trails Illustrated Topo Map 228; *Map 10, Appalachian Trail and Other Trails in Shenandoah National Park, Central District* (PATC, Inc.)

The Hike

The trailhead to South River Falls is to the right of the drinking fountain at the South River picnic area. The trail descends gradually for 0.1 mile to a junction with the Appalachian Trail. A cement post orients you to the surrounding features. Milam Gap and Swift Run Gap are 11.5 miles and 3 miles to the southwest, respectively.

Continue your hike from the post following the blue blazes, and begin a series of gradual switchbacks as you descend the trail. In places the trail is rocky, but it is wide and, for the most part, smooth until it approaches the first of several creeks that combine to create South River. In the past hikers have attempted to save time by cutting across the trail, creating erosion. As a result, the park stipulates via several signs that hikers remain on the trail.

At about 0.75 mile you will encounter another creek entering from the left. It is difficult to see because it runs beneath the rocks, but it certainly is audible. Just past the creek are a number of trees downed by the strong winds of a September 1996 storm. Though rot is working its magic of absorption, huge unstable ghosts persist, vaguely obscured in places by a vigorous forest understory. Other creeks continue to flow from the left into the South River, which parallels the trail as it continues its descent.

Just a few yards past the juncture of the creek, the South River plunges dramatically downward into a great hollow. It is difficult to see the falls until you approach a natural overlook, at 1.3 miles. *Caution:* Do not get too close to the edge. A few yards farther along the trail, cement walls provide a more protected spot from which to view the falls below you. (**Option:** At this point you may turn around and retrace your steps, making this a 2.6-mile hike.)

To continue the 4.4-mile hike, the trail joins an old road that comes in from the left at 1.5 miles. The road leads northwest to the South River Falls Fire Road. However, continue along the widening South River Falls Trail, which was once used by inhabitants traveling from one hollow to another. This wider trail descends, then swings back toward the base of the falls and a cement post encircled by an aluminum band at 2.1 miles. The post states that it is 0.3 mile to the end of the road and the park's boundary with the Virginia Wildlife Management Area. It also advises you of the existence of a short spur trail to the fall's base about 0.1 mile away. At 2.2 miles take the narrow spur trail. You may have to scurry over downed trees.

At 83 feet South River Falls is the park's third-highest fall. Wading in the refreshing pool at its base would be invigorating on a hot summer day—all the better to prepare you for the challenging hike back up to the trailhead.

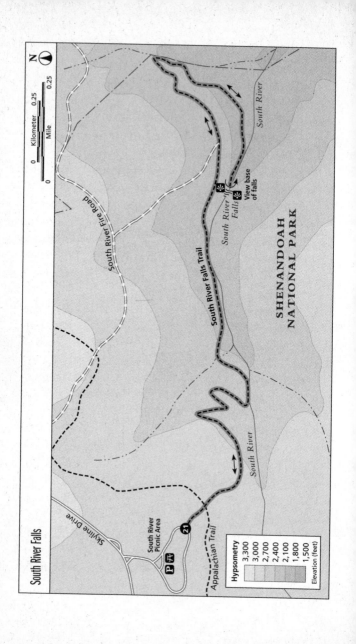

South River Falls

Miles and Directions

0.0 Trailhead located past drinking fountain at South River picnic area; descend.

0.1 Cross AT and continue descent on South River Falls Trail following the blue blazes.

0.75 Stream running beneath rocks.

1.3 Overlook for South River Falls; continue toward the east. (**Option:** Turn around and retrace your steps for a hike of 2.6 miles.)

1.5 Junction with old road.

2.1 Cement post; path from trail to spur trail.

2.2 Spur trail to South River Falls; retrace steps back to trailhead.

4.4 Arrive at trailhead.

South District

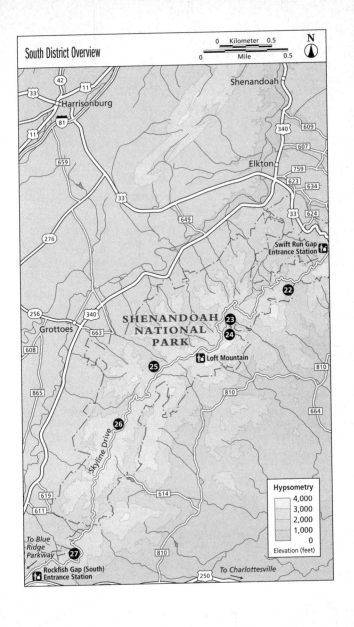

22 Powell Gap

This is an Appalachian Trail leg stretcher that leads to a rock overlook offering excellent views of Powell Gap Hollow and the mountains and farmlands to the east.

Start: Skyline Drive Mile 70.0, at sign for Powell Gap; park along east side of road near small meadow
Trailhead GPS: N38 19.2732' / W78 35.53380'
Type of hike: Out and back
Distance: 1.0 mile
Hiking time: 30 to 60 minutes
Difficulty: Moderate

Elevation gain and loss: 300 to 400 feet
Canine compatibility: Dogs allowed
Maps: National Geographic Trails Illustrated Topo Map 228; *Map 11, Appalachian Trail and Other Trails in Shenandoah National Park, South District* (PATC, Inc.)

The Hike

On a late fall or early winter day, this hike could lead to some spectacular views. This is one of our favorite short hikes.

Access the trail by walking to the cement post adjacent to the "Powell Gap" sign. This hike follows the Appalachian Trail south. It begins to climb immediately, gradually but steadily; it peaks at 0.5 mile, at a short spur trail that provides an overlook to the east. After soaking in the countryside and, if you are lucky, some sun, turn around and retrace your steps to the trailhead.

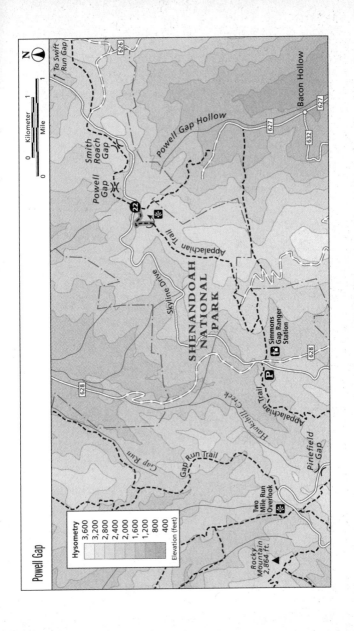

Powell Gap

Miles and Directions

0.0 Cement post on east side of Skyline Drive; follow AT south.

0.5 Spur trail to rock ledge overlook; turn around, retrace steps.

1.0 Arrive at cement post.

23 Ivy Creek

An out-and-back hike containing some moderate and a few more challenging segments that concludes at the Loft Mountain Campground.

Start: Skyline Drive Mile 77.5, Ivy Creek Overlook; access the Appalachian Trail from south end of parking lot at cement post (white blazes)
Trailhead GPS: N38 17.082' / W78 39.5445'
Type of hike: Out and back
Distance: 2.8 miles
Hiking time: 2 to 3 hours

Difficulty: Moderate
Elevation loss and gain: 695 feet
Canine compatibility: Dogs allowed
Maps: National Geographic Trails Illustrated Topo Map 228; *Map 11, Appalachian Trail and Other Trails in Shenandoah National Park, South District* (PATC, Inc.)

The Hike

The hike begins on the south side of the Ivy Creek Overlook. Turn south onto the AT and begin a gradual descent amid sassafras, laurel, oak, and pine. The trail then begins to climb and makes several switchbacks, passing by several large boulders. Soon, there will be beautiful views to the east of Loft Mountain. In late summer the trail is flanked by mint, goldenrod, and yellow daisies. In winter the trail is open and spacious and provides seemingly unending views.

At 0.7 mile the trail reaches a rock outcropping on the left from which you can see Skyline Drive and Patterson Ridge below. (**Option:** Turn around here if you are tired or time is short.) To continue, start downhill amid blueberries—a food source popular with bears.

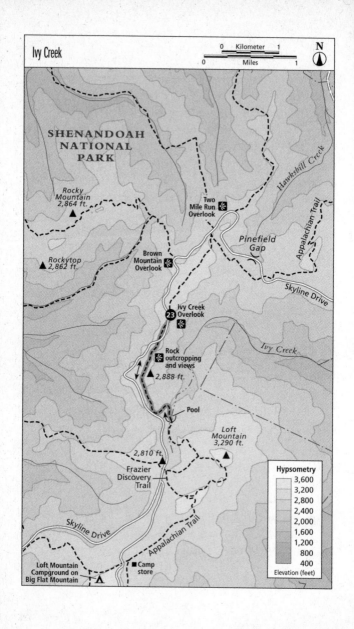

Ivy Creek

SHENANDOAH
NATIONAL
PARK

Rocky
Mountain
2,864 ft.

Rockytop
2,862 ft.

Two
Mile Run
Overlook

Hawksbill Creek

Pinefield
Gap

Appalachian Trail

Brown
Mountain
Overlook

Skyline Drive

Ivy Creek
Overlook

Ivy Creek

Rock
outcropping
and views

2,888 ft.

Pool

Loft
Mountain
3,290 ft.

2,810 ft.

Frazier
Discovery
Trail

Skyline Drive

Appalachian Trail

Loft Mountain
Campground on
Big Flat Mountain

Camp
store

Hypsometry

3,600
3,200
2,800
2,400
2,000
1,600
1,200
800
400

Elevation (feet)

0   Kilometer   1
0   Miles   1

N

As the trail continues its descent, Ivy Creek is on the left at 1.4 miles. Here, there is also a beautiful, small pool—a nice spot to rest and snack. This is the only place in the park where the AT parallels a stream for any considerable distance. Enjoy, then turn around and return the way you came.

Miles and Directions

0.0 Ivy Creek Overlook; turn south onto the AT.

0.7 Rock outcropping and views.

1.4 Ivy Creek and pool; turn around, retrace steps.

2.8 Arrive at Ivy Creek Overlook.

24 Loft Mountain Loop

This fun family hike to the northeast summit of Loft Mountain offers views at several places.

Start: Skyline Drive Mile 79.5, Loft Mountain Wayside parking lot
Trailhead GPS: N38 15.858' / W78 39.575'
Type of hike: Loop
Distance: 2.7 miles
Hiking time: About 2 hours
Difficulty: Easy
Elevation gain and loss: About 600 feet

Canine compatibility: Dogs allowed on all trails except Frazier Discovery Trail
Maps: National Geographic Trails Illustrated Topo Map 228; *Map 11, Appalachian Trail and Other Trails in Shenandoah National Park, South District* (PATC, Inc.)

The Hike

This is a very enjoyable hike and one that is suitable for the whole family.

From the wayside parking lot, walk north on Skyline Drive for about 150 yards. Pass the trailhead for the Patterson Ridge Trail (a one-way trail) on the left. Turn right onto the first dirt road, and proceed to the Ivy Creek hut, which serves as a PATC Maintenance Building, and the Ivy Creek Spring at 0.4 mile. A cement post marks the junction with the Appalachian Trail at 0.6 mile. Turn right and ascend through hardwood forest following white blazes.

As you approach the summit of Loft Mountain, the trees grow more sparsely and blackberry bushes abound. At 1 mile the trail levels out on the ridgetop and continues to an overlook with rock outcroppings on the left side of the trail

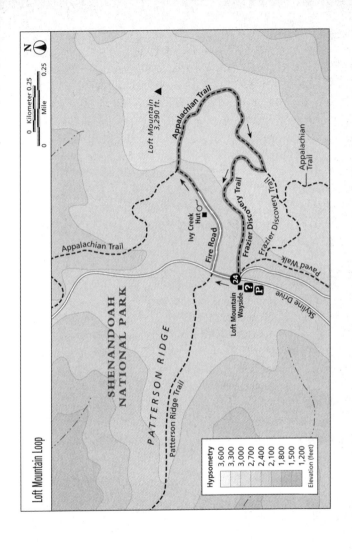

Loft Mountain Loop

at 1.1 miles. From here you get a lovely 180-degree view to the east of the Piedmont (on clear days); to the left is Flattop Mountain, and to the right is Fox Mountain with three peaks, a hollow, then two more peaks. The valley below is pastoral, and you can watch clouds and storms roll in. Also along the ridgetop are fields of yarrow and more berry bushes.

At the next cement post at 1.4 miles, turn right on the Frazier Discovery Trail and prepare yourself for a number of stunning views and for a hike along some incredible rock outcroppings. This portion of the trail is 1.3 miles long and will return you to the Loft Mountain Wayside, which is about 100 yards from your trailhead but should be where you parked your vehicle.

Miles and Directions

0.0 Loft Mountain Wayside parking lot; follow Skyline Drive north for 150 yards to dirt fire road on right. About 60 yards down the trail, cement post on right. Turn right onto dirt road; ascend.

0.4 Cement post, Ivy Creek hut, and spring; follow blue blazes uphill, cross small creek.

0.6 Cement post; junction with AT; turn right onto AT and follow white blazes uphill.

1.0 Trail levels on ridgetop.

1.1 Overlook on left.

1.4 Cement post; turn right onto Frazier Discovery Trail.

1.5 Undesignated side trail to right leading to overlook; follow the Frazier Discovery Trail for another 1.2 miles down to the trailhead on Skyline Drive.

2.7 Arrive at Loft Mountain Wayside parking lot.

25 Blackrock Summit

A short loop hike brings you to a spectacular rocky summit with a short boulder scramble at the top.

Start: Skyline Drive Mile 84.8, Blackrock parking lot
Trailhead GPS: N38 13.16' / W78 44.371'
Type of hike: Loop
Distance: 1.0 mile
Hiking time: 30 to 60 minutes
Difficulty: Easy
Elevation gain and loss: 175 feet

Canine compatibility: Dogs allowed
Maps: National Geographic Trails Illustrated Topo Map 228; *Map 11, Appalachian Trail and Other Trails in Shenandoah National Park, South District* (PATC, Inc.)
Special consideration: This is a "Kids Track Trail," a national park program that enhances the hike for children.

The Hike

This a great hike for families. The trailhead is located at a sign in the Blackrock parking lot that interprets the mountain's geology. After reading it, ascend rather sharply on the Trayfoot Mountain Trail to its junction with the Appalachian Trail at 0.1 mile. Take the AT left (south), following the white blazes. The AT remains level almost all the way to the summit.

At 0.5 mile the trail stops just short of the summit. To reach Blackrock Summit, you must scramble a short distance over a jumble of boulders, but the view makes the climb worth it. *Caution:* Occasionally, hikers report seeing rattlesnakes sunning themselves on the rocks, so watch where you step!

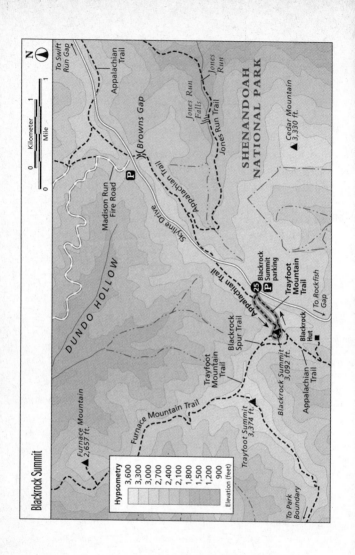

Blackrock Summit

From the summit you can see Buzzard Rock and Trayfoot, Horsehead, and Furnace Mountains. On a very clear day, try to locate Hightop Mountain. (**Option:** From the summit, you can take an easy trail northwest to Trayfoot Summit [another 0.7 mile away], where there are the remains of an old fire tower, but you won't get any good views.)

Blackrock Summit played an unusual role in Virginia history. During the Revolutionary War, Virginia governor Thomas Jefferson was reportedly concerned about the safety of the Great Seal of Virginia and the state archives. He gave them to a friend, who hid them in a cave at Blackrock until the war's end.

The hike continues, following the AT south around Blackrock Summit to another cement post at 0.6 mile. On the post an arrow points left to the old road that is now part of Trayfoot Mountain Trail (blue blazes), which leads back to the trailhead.

Miles and Directions

0.0 Blackrock parking lot; ascend on Trayfoot Mountain Trail.

0.1 Intersection with AT; take AT south (white blazes).

0.5 Blackrock Summit.

0.6 Intersection of AT and Trayfoot Mountain Trail; follow Trayfoot (blue blazes) back to parking lot.

1.0 Arrive at Blackrock parking lot.

26 **Calvary and Chimney Rocks**

Despite its 3-plus miles, this is a relatively easy family hike to interesting geological formations.

Start: Skyline Drive Mile 90.0, Riprap parking lot on west side of Skyline Drive
Trailhead GPS: N38 10.670' / W78 45.911'
Type of hike: Out and back
Distance: 3.2 miles
Hiking time: 2 to 3 hours
Difficulty: Easy

Elevation gain and loss: About 850 feet
Canine compatibility: Dogs allowed
Maps: National Geographic Trails Illustrated Topo Map 228; *Map 11, Appalachian Trail and Other Trails in Shenandoah National Park, South District* (PATC, Inc.)

The Hike

This 3.2-mile hike is moderately easy and one of the prettiest hikes in the park. Much of it is through a designated wilderness area.

From the end of the Riprap parking lot, take the Appalachian Trail north and follow the white blazes. Climb under a canopy of oak, maple, and sassafras before reaching a cement post at the junction with the Riprap Trail at 0.4 mile. Go left (west), following the blue blazes. Now the trail is lined with blueberry bushes. It heads downhill via switchbacks, then climbs to a knoll jumbled with lichen-covered rocks and boulders—a jumble known as *riprap*.

At 0.7 mile you reach a saddle, then almost immediately you are provided with great views of the seemingly infinite talus slope and Paine Run Watershed. The striated boulders are Erwin quartzite, as are the rocks at Calvary Rocks and

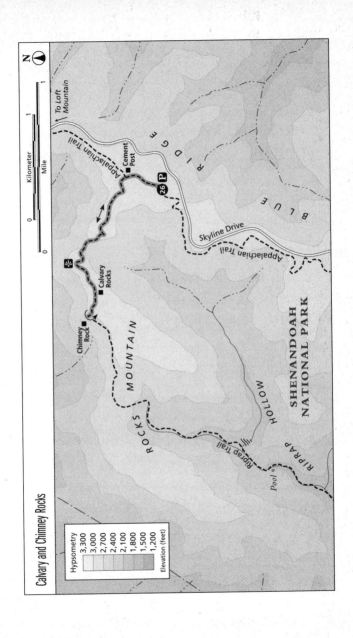

Calvary and Chimney Rocks

Hypsometry

Elevation (feet)
- 3,300
- 3,000
- 2,700
- 2,400
- 2,100
- 1,800
- 1,500
- 1,200

N

Kilometer

Mile

To Loft Mountain

Appalachian Trail

Cement Post

26 P

BLUE RIDGE

Skyline Drive

Appalachian Trail

Calvary Rocks

Chimney Rock

ROCKS MOUNTAIN

Riprap Trail

HOLLOW

RIPRAP

Pool

SHENANDOAH NATIONAL PARK

Chimney Rock, not far ahead. Follow the ridgetop up and down to Calvary Rocks at 1.4 miles, which offer a good northwest view. Continue to Chimney Rock at 1.6 miles. Iron pegs imbedded in the rock are part of an old bridge. Again, you have a good view to the west.

From this point, turn around and retrace your steps to the Riprap parking lot. (**Option:** After Chimney Rock the narrow trail levels, and there are a couple more small lookout points. Then it begins a gentle descent off the ridge and back into the forest before descending steeply for several more miles to the park boundary. Explore as far as you'd like.)

Miles and Directions

0.0 Cement post at Riprap parking lot.

0.4 Cement post; turn left, following blue blazes.

0.7 Saddle, then great views created in part by the extensive talus slope.

1.4 Calvary Rocks.

1.6 Chimney Rock; turn around, retrace steps.

3.2 Arrive at Riprap parking lot.

27 Calf Mountain

This pleasant hike to the top of Calf Mountain winds through old pastures and some new-growth trees.

Start: Skyline Drive Mile 99.5, Beagle Gap parking area on east side of Skyline Drive
Trailhead GPS: N38 05.762' / W78 46.819'
Type of hike: Out and back
Distance: 2.0 miles
Hiking time: 1 to 2 hours
Difficulty: Easy

Elevation gain and loss: 443 feet
Canine compatibility: Dogs allowed
Maps: National Geographic Trails Illustrated Topo Map 228; *Map 11, Appalachian Trail and Other Trails in Shenandoah National Park, South District* (PATC, Inc.)

The Hike

This short climb up Calf Mountain is delightful, partly because the trail winds through old meadows rather than through woods, giving you a chance to see more of the landscape. The dirt trail is well maintained. In summer, if it is hot and humid, you might want to hike this one early or late in the day.

Walk through the V opening in the wire fence with white blazes on it, and ascend through a meadow filled with wildflowers and berry bushes to the Appalachian Trail going north, which enters a small stand of new-growth trees and bushes and quickly gets steeper. Then it levels out and leads through meadows to a large stand of old but still-bearing apple trees—the remnants of an introduced apple orchard. In autumn, near the periphery of the old pasture land, sumac bushes can be lush with dark-red berries.

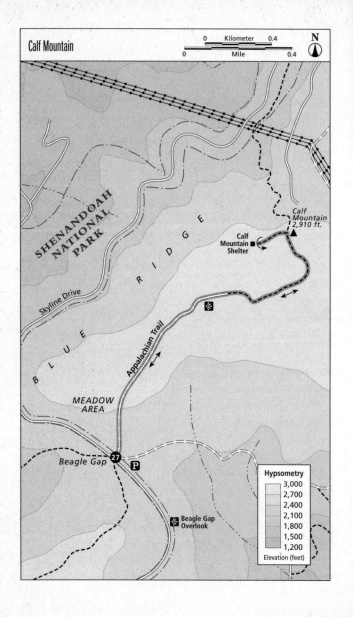

Calf Mountain

Shenandoah National Park

Blue Ridge

Skyline Drive

Appalachian Trail

Calf Mountain 2,910 ft.

Calf Mountain Shelter

Meadow Area

Beagle Gap

27

P

Beagle Gap Overlook

Hypsometry	
3,000	
2,700	
2,400	
2,100	
1,800	
1,500	
1,200	

Elevation (feet)

0   Kilometer   0.4
0   Mile   0.4

N

At 0.7 mile there is a good view to the east. You are not at the summit yet. At 1.0 mile you will know you've reached the top if you begin to descend on logs and rocks placed across the trail. From the summit, you can wander on as far as time allows and then retrace your route to the parking lot, and enjoy, once again, the area's openness and lush vegetation.

Miles and Directions

0.0   Beagle Gap parking lot. Walk through a V opening in wire fence with white blaze.

0.7   View.

1.0   Summit of Calf Mountain; retrace steps.

2.0   Arrive at Beagle Gap parking lot.

About the Authors

Bert Gildart has been writing about the outdoors for more than thirty years. He served as a backcountry ranger in Glacier National Park over thirteen summers. He has written more than 300 magazine articles for such publications as *Smithsonian, Travel & Leisure, Modern Maturity, Field & Stream,* and *National Wildlife.*

Together, Bert and his wife, Janie, have hiked thousands of miles throughout many wilderness and backcountry areas of the United States. They have collaborated on many other FalconGuides, including: *Hiking Shenandoah National Park, A FalconGuide to Death Valley National Park, A FalconGuide to Dinosaur National Monument, Best Easy Day Hikes Black Hills Country,* and *Hiking the Black Hills Country.* Bert has also authored two books of his essays and photographs entitled *Montana Icons* and *Glacier Icons.* As photographers, their stock files number well over 100,000; samples can be seen at GildartPhoto.com.